A Journey In
The Prophetic

Prophetic Words from the Throne of Grace

Find Understanding, Purpose, Peace & Destiny
As You Walk from Religion to Relationship
Come With Me, On A Journey in the Prophetic…

ristie

D1367749

A Journey In The Prophetic
Copyright © 2011 by Wendy M Christie
All Rights Reserved

Table of Contents

From The Author

Hello, my name is Wendy M Christie. I am in love with Jesus, my wonderful husband, my five beautiful children and living. I always strive to stay present every moment so I can enjoy the great people and things that God has given me. Above all, I try to keep a grateful heart in all things.

I have been writing Prophetic Words for about five years now. The Lord told me to write a book and at first I was impatient for it, but the Lord has His perfect timing. Finally, the time is NOW. The Sons of God are manifesting in the earth now and God is moving in the Body of Christ like never before. Many who think they have the truth will be shocked and very disappointed that they have put their hope in a building, a ministry, a Pastor, themselves or other things. These other people and things were not anointed to 'carry' our Hope. When we finally redirect our Hope to Jesus, we CAN NOT and WILL NOT be disappointed. A paramount part of our walk with God is hearing His voice. We must hear His voice with the 'Ears of True Understanding', so we CAN be Spirit led. Being Spirit led is what takes us from the burden of the law, into the FREEDOM and REST of His Grace.

The Bible says that the truth shall set us FREE. Sometimes that Truth can be a painful thing for us to face. But the Lord said, **"Now is the time for FREEDOM!"**

You will not be able to read this Book without being changed. The Lord told me that this book is a Journey, and as you walk through this Journey with me, you will come to the place of Freedom and Revelation that He has brought me to in my walk with Him. You may see a date on each Word, but the Word is for you when you read it and receive it - there is no space or time in the Spirit realm.

Lord, I pray that the Spirit of Truth, Wisdom, Revelation and Understanding fall on Your people and allow them to receive the gift that You are giving them through this book. In Jesus Name, Amen...

Acknowledgments

First, ALL Glory, in ALL things in my life goes to **God**. Without Him I am nothing. He is the greatest love of my life.

I would like to dedicate this Book to and give special recognition to my Husband, **Chad Christie**. He contributed so much to this book, whether it was in finding scriptures, giving insight, editing or prophetic revelation. Thank you Honey for all your help, love, patience and support. I couldn't be me without you. I Love You!

To my **Parents** and my **Mother-in-law**, thank you for all your help, love and support, I love you all!

I would like to thank my dear friend **Linda Marie Irish**. She is the author of the book, "It's A God Thing... MY SHEEP WILL HEAR MY VOICE." She believed in me and was a paramount part of nudging me to make this vision that the Lord gave me a reality! Thank you for your friendship, love and support dear Linda!

To the many wonderful people of God who support me in the online ministry, on Facebook - you have helped me keep going with all of your prayers and encouragement, thank you, I love you all and God Bless!

To my enemies, you were actually my greatest teachers and allies in life. Thank you, I love you and God Bless!

Tips On How To Read This Book

To better prepare you for my writing style, let me elaborate a little on how to read this book. The **Prophetic Words** will require your (and God's) interpretation as well as understanding (just ask God if you are struggling with the interpretation part). So you know who is saying what, and where scripture starts and ends, the book legend is as follows...

When God is Speaking the text is, **"Bolded and in Quotes."** It will also say, "The Lord said" before it or it will say, "Says the Lord of Hosts," or something similar, at the beginning and end of it.

Important Words or Points are also bolded. You will also notice that my writing style has many capitalized letters - this is for an emphasis on importance as well.

Scripture References are Italicized and will have the Version of the Bible listed at the end of them (e.g. MKJV - This is the Modern King James Version). All versions of the Bible that are used in this Book are listed on the permissions page in the beginning of the Book. If you see scriptures that are *Italicized* and then you see (non-italicized words in parenthesis) within the scripture, that is me talking or shedding a little more light on the verse.

I recommend **NOT** 'Racing' through this book... Although you may be able to read much and retain much, God has his perfect timing and He may intend a certain Word for you at a certain time, without the weight of several other Words competing for your full attention. As you get into this book, you will find that there is a lot of **'meat'** in these **Prophetic Words.** It is probably a good idea to pause and reflect after every word (like chewing your meat thoroughly), to see how it relates to you and your circumstances. Quite often a Word is not actually for someone until they 'Receive' it. Once you decide, "That is FOR ME! I Receive THAT!" All of a sudden, YES, it is for you...

Dates that are listed under the title of each Word are the dates that the Lord gave me different revelations regarding these Words. Most of them were mostly complete on the first date listed, and the other dates listed are revision dates when I may have gotten a little more revelation on the Word (or for editing purposes). The dates that say 'Released' in front of them are the dates that God had me release the Word. If there is just one date, that was the date that the Word was written (some of the earlier Words were not released, until now).

Also, throughout this book, you will see opportunities to read a passage, complete an action, ponder something or maybe even take some notes. Please do yourself a favor and take a little extra time in these instances, and, do not be afraid to follow directions, even if they seem silly or unnecessary. Surely anything God tells us to do, we would do, right? Practicing this, whether from God, our boss, a parent or someone else, will help us to see certain things and gain important knowledge with regards to much of what you will encounter in this book. Plus, listening to God and following directions often reveals hidden blessing.

May God bless you on your Journey...

THE PURSUIT OF HAPPINESS VS TRUE HAPPINESS

6/15/2010

The Pursuit of Happiness will always be just that - a Pursuit. Happiness is not something we find outside of ourselves, but rather something we discover was there in our hearts all along. We have all been conditioned to think that if something turns out differently than we thought it would, that we are somehow supposed to be upset, angry or unhappy. We actually have the power to recondition ourselves to another way of thinking - to see everything that comes our way as a gift that was brought into our lives to teach us, mature us and give us the opportunity to learn how to **TRUST IN GOD**. Taking our HOPE out of the things and circumstances of our lives and putting it **IN CHRIST** is where **True Peace** is found. Happiness can then be a decision that no matter what is happening to you, you can be happy. So, decide to **JUST BE HAPPY!**

THE LITTLE CAGED BIRD

2/9/2011

God gave me an analogy that was so simple, yet so profound. He gave me a vision of a little caged bird. It was injured and it was crying out for help. The Lord said, **"Sometimes, My people are this little bird."** Isn't that just like us to put ourselves in a little cage and God in a little box? The little bird kept hopping around on its perch and squawking for help. "Chirp, chirp, chirp," said the little bird. Then the huge hand reached into the cage to Give the little bird some Help. The little bird did not SEE the large hand as help. In fact, this Hand seemed to be an enemy, or something that would hurt it. So, the little bird began to thrash itself about, in the cage, trying to avoid the **BIG HAND**, all along injuring itself even more in the process. The little bird continued to **FREAK OUT** in fear of the BIG HAND. You see, this is the way we are sometimes. God's **BIG HAND OF HELP** sometimes looks like 'the devil' or our enemy, but in fact it is God in His Infinite Wisdom uprooting us and trying to plant us on the Solid Ground. **Trust IN HIM; it is the Secret Place - our place of Provision and Protection**. Trust IN HIM will help us in ALL of life, to stop 'Freaking Out' and **REST IN HIS PEACE and GRACE...**

Scripture References

No temptation has taken you but what is common to man; but God is faithful, who will not allow you to be tempted above what you are able, but with the temptation also will make a way to escape, so that you may be able to bear it. (1 Corinthians 10:13 MKJV)

He who dwells in the secret place of the Most High shall rest under the shadow of the Almighty. I will say of Jehovah, my refuge and my fortress; my God; in Him I will trust. (Psalm 91:1-2 MKJV)

RESURRECTION, ENLARGEMENT, ELEVATION, I AM ENLARGING YOU SO YOU WILL BE ABLE TO RECEIVE WHAT I AM BRINGING

4/5/2007

"For I will bring those things that have been dead on the inside to life again. There will be life, where there once was complacency, fear, heaviness and blindness. Those things will be lifting from you and a release is coming. So get ready, a great release is coming. Like a flood will I pour out My Spirit and heal your families, your finances, your homes, your hearts, your minds and your testimony. I will lift the blinders and you will see further and further into the future and into the deep things of My Spirit, for I have appointed this time and this place to be as a landmark and witness to the great and wondrous workings I will do to you and through you, if you Submit to My Spirit, Humble yourself, Pray, Seek My Face, and allow Me to do what I have said** (What He is describing here is RELATIONSHIP). **Do not fear for I am with you. Neither will I leave you, nor will I forsake you, says the Lord of Hosts."

I see the Lord holding His hand out saying, **"You can trust me. Do you trust me?"**

Scripture References

*If my people, which are called by my name, shall **humble themselves, and pray, and seek my face, and turn from their wicked ways; then will I hear from heaven, and will forgive their sin, and will heal** (heal here is the Hebrew word rapha raphah - meaning wholeness) their land* (territory). *Now mine eyes shall be open, and mine ears attend unto the prayer that is made in this place. For now have I chosen and sanctified this house that my name may be there for ever: and mine eyes and mine heart shall be there perpetually* (eternally). (2 Chronicles 7:14-16 KJV)

IN THE SPIRIT OF DAVID, DANCE BEFORE THE LORD & RELEASE THE GENERATIONAL BLESSING OF ABRAHAM

4/5/2007

And the Lord said, **"Restoration; I am putting things back into alignment."** I keep seeing a warrior inside of God's people and this warrior is breaking out of their chests and he is carrying a harpoon and he is shooting and hitting and pulling things back to God's people - those things that the enemy has stolen from them. He is also beginning to overtake everything about them. The inside man is overtaking the outside man by force - this is a forceful thing, a 'wrestling with God' kind of thing. *And from the days of John the Baptist until now the kingdom of heaven suffered violence, and the violent take it by force.* (Matthew 11:12 KJV) Here, violent means - intense passion, and by force means, literally, to snatch away - they will 'Take it.' We are taking our **lives** back by force! The Lord is calling us to 'violence' in and throughout the spirit realm, to war in the Spirit, on our behalf and on the behalf of others, to take back what the enemy has stripped from us and other people. *No one was missing--young or old, sons or daughters. David brought back everything that had been stolen,* (1 Samuel 30:19 CEV)

I also keep seeing sparkles all over and around the people of God like stars flashing. I see a vision of Abraham and the stars and the Generational Blessing - The New Covenant. The Lord is bringing about the fullness of, and restoring us to The New Covenant IN Him.

In the Spirit of David - Dance before the Lord And Release the Generational Blessing!

UNITY & RESPECT FOR AUTHORITY & FOR OTHERS EQUALS PEACE & POSSIBILITY

4/8/2007

I was at a Christian event, and it was like I was **looking in** from the outside at all of the people fellowshipping and loving on each other, and God gave me a glimpse of the potential for unity in the hearts of His people. He said, **"These people have the possibility to be in such unity, that No Thing would ever be impossible for them. I am beginning to Fine Tune That Unity. Do NOT put limits on MY Spirit. I am willing to do exceedingly, abundantly and above ALL that you could hope, ask or think, according to the power that works on the inside of you. The same power that raised Christ from the dead is working on the inside of you. The only limitation that is ever present is the limitation that you have in our own mind."** *For as he thinketh in his heart, so is he...* (Proverbs 23:7 KJV)

Whatever we can believe for, **HE IS ABLE** to do. Aim high with your expectations and don't limit God. His 'unified' body of believers is a people that He can trust - a people with His very own heartbeat. The Lord said, **"Stay in unity, especially in the area of respect for authority, the anointing flows from the top down."** If we are putting a kink in the garden hose, so to speak, no flow can get through. So, stay in unity and **respect for others, especially in respect for authority**, and nothing will ever be impossible for you. Not out of self-motivation or selfish motives, but ALL for His Glory, His Namesake and His purposes in the earth.

And the Lord said, **"If you want peace in your life, you need to be properly aligned with authority and properly aligned with others,** (horizontal and vertical) **there can be no disorder, no turmoil, no confusion, and no anarchy."** God has a protocol, etiquette or code of behavior that we must follow if we want to be in alignment to be bless-able, and to be able to receive from Him. If there is a lack of peace in your life, take a look at your respect for authority, and for others. God will help you if you need help - just ask Him. Don't worry, He loves you and He is with you. One major part of respecting God's ORDER is to understand his True Order of Authority first. The Order of Authority in the earth realm is this - **Apostle, Prophet, Evangelist, Pastor, Teacher** - in that order. If this Order is not recognized and respected, disunity will follow. Is any one of these better than the other? No, we all have our part in the Body of Christ, but we must recognize God's Order, this is a point of obedience in His eyes and He will bless us for it. We are not to regard man or man's system as above God, God's Word or God's unseen realm, for his Order is and unseen thing.

I understand that many people have fallen prey to leaders or authorities who would take advantage or abuse those who are under their authority. This is wrong. In these cases, seek the Lord and be Spirit led. Ask the Lord if you should remove yourself from a situation such as this. Sometimes you have to make hard decisions for your own safety. Seek God and He will lead you and guide you through. The Lord is separating the wheat from the tares, at this point in History. The point is, we have to **BE SPIRIT LED** in all things and in all ways. If we are, we will be in the place that the Lord wants us to be, when He wants us to be there. Then, He is responsible for the outcome. We can trust that if He said to do something, that He has an outcome in mind and He is For us. *But whom He predestinated, these He also called; and whom He called, those He also justified. And whom He justified, these He also glorified. What then shall we say to these things? If God is for us, who can be against us? Truly He who did not spare His own Son, but delivered Him up for us all, how shall He not with Him also freely give us all things? Who shall lay anything to the charge of God's elect? It is God who justifies.* (Romans 8:30-33 MKJV)

Scripture References

With all lowliness (humbleness) *and meekness, with longsuffering, forbearing one another in love; Endeavouring to keep the* **unity of the Spirit in the bond of peace.** *There is one body, and one Spirit, even as ye are called in one hope of your calling; One Lord, one faith, one baptism, One God and Father of all, who is above all, and through all, and in you all. But unto every one of us is given grace according to the measure of the gift of Christ. Wherefore he saith, When he ascended up on high, he led captivity captive,* **and gave gifts unto men.** *(Now that he ascended, what is it but that he also descended first into the lower parts of the earth? He that descended is the same also that ascended up far above all heavens, that he might fill all things.) And he gave some,* **apostles;** *and some,* **prophets;** *and some,* **evangelists;** *and some,* **pastors** *and* **teachers;** *For the* **perfecting** (maturing) *of the saints, for the work of the ministry, for the edifying of the body of Christ: Till we all come in the* **unity of the faith, and of the knowledge of the Son of God,** *unto a perfect man, unto the measure of the stature of the fulness of Christ: That we henceforth be no more children, tossed to and fro, and carried about with every wind of doctrine, by the sleight of men, and cunning craftiness, whereby they lie in wait to deceive; But speaking the truth in love, may* **grow up into him in all things, which is the head,** *even Christ: From whom the whole body fitly joined together and compacted by that which every joint supplieth, according to the effectual working in the measure of every part, maketh increase of the body unto the edifying of itself in love.* (Ephesians 4:2-16 KJV)

Obey your leaders and do what they say. They are watching over you, and they must answer to God. So don't make them sad as they do their work. Make them happy. Otherwise, they won't be able to help you at all. (Hebrews 13:17 CEV)

And the LORD said, "Behold, they are one people, and they have all one language, and this is only the beginning of what they will do. And nothing that they propose to do will now be impossible for them." (Genesis 11:6 CEV)

Now unto him that is able to do exceeding abundantly above all that we ask or think, according to the power that works in us, (Ephesians 3:20 KJV)

*But if the Spirit of him that raised up Jesus from the dead dwell in you, he that raised up Christ from the dead shall also **quicken your mortal bodies by his Spirit that dwells in you**.* (Romans 8:11 KJV)

Again I say unto you, that if two of you shall agree on earth as touching any thing that they shall ask, it shall be done for them of my Father which is in heaven. For where two or three are gathered together in my name, there am I in the midst of them. (Matthew 18:19-20 KJV)

THE CLAP OF THUNDER, BRINGING
ALL THINGS INTO ALIGNMENT

4/15/2007

I had a vision about Intercessory Prayer. We are standing in the middle of two opposing opinions pleading someone's case, just like a lawyer might. The **power** lies between two opposing opinions. In the natural, the Heavens are positively charged and the earth is negatively charged and the only way to bring things **back into balance** is for a thunderstorm to happen. God gave me a vision that was very simple about Intercessory Prayer...

In the diagram below, God is up in Heaven, people are below on the earth, His intercessors are in the middle...

_____ **God** (in Heaven) _____

This Creates **Power** In The Atmosphere...

God has given **His Intercessors** this power...

____ **People** (who need us to intercede on their behalf) ____

Then I heard God say, **"The CLAP of thunder brings everything back into alignment, or balance."** Our voices in the earthly realm hold this POWER, the same as a clap of thunder.

It is the storms that bring balance to our lives.

I also remembered a scripture about God's voice being like thunder...

Listen carefully to the thunder of His voice, and the rumbling that comes out of His mouth. (Job 37:2 MKJV)

INTERNAL SIEGE - IT IS THE SWORD OF THE LORD, THAT SLAYS THE GREAT MEN

4/11/2007

When I would minister and lay hands on people, God would often have me clap my hands. I didn't know why, so I asked God to show me in the Bible where this was...

My husband, Chad, found this scripture and gave it to me. *You therefore, son of man, prophesy, And strike your hands together. The third time let the sword do double damage. It is the sword that slays, the sword that slays the great men, that enters their private chambers.* (Ezekiel 21:14 NKJV™)

Internal siege - The Lord keeps saying to me, **"Internal Siege."**

Does this mean that every time I minister to people that I legalistically clap my hands? No, I only clap my hands in obedience. The Lord knows what He is doing - we simply follow Him and obey. **Always, only be Spirit led in ALL things and in all ways,** then He will make your path a straight one. *Trust in Jehovah with all your heart, and lean not to your own understanding. In all your ways acknowledge Him, and He shall direct your paths.* (Proverbs 3:5-6 MKJV)

The Lord told me that when I obeyed Him, and clapped, no matter how silly I may have looked, it was an act of faith in obedience to Him. Then He would bring things into alignment in people's souls and their natural bodies. He said that their spirits are already in alignment, because our spirits are tiny pieces of what God is, and He is perfect. It is our souls and our bodies that need healing. He also told me that this 'clapping' was applying His sword, the very Word of the Lord, to their souls and their physical bodies. Then, when the sword is applied, it cuts through and divides the soul from the spirit, the joints from the marrow and discerns the thoughts and intents of the heart of a person. *For the Word of God is living and powerful and sharper than any two-edged sword, piercing even to the dividing apart of soul and spirit, and of the joints and marrow, and is a discerner of the thoughts and intents of the heart. Neither is there any creature that is not manifest in His sight, but all things are naked and opened to the eyes of Him with whom we have to do.* (Hebrews 4:12-13 MKJV)

Later, when I started ministering to people more often, the Lord would tell me to clap. And, it was **then**, when He would reveal to me what it was that I needed to say or pray for that person. The Lord would also begin to let me see things about the person that I could not have possibly known - this elevates their faith level, their faith makes them whole, see Mark 5:34. In the spirit realm, the instant His sword is applied over that person, there is a transformation that happens (sometimes the physical realm takes some time to catch up).

THERE WILL BE A CHANGING OF THE GUARD, THE WATCHMAN RISES

4/21/2007

And the Lord said, **"The Watchman Rises."** Here, rises means goes up, increases, and makes something larger in number, quantity, or degree.

He also said, "**There will be a Changing** (shifting) **of the Guard"**. The **Watchman,** and the **Watchman Prophet** is the Guard He is speaking of (there are some that carry the **Watchmen** anointing and there are also some **Prophets** that carry the **Watchmen** anointing).

And the Lord said, **"The Watchman will be the Magistrate."** The **Magistrate** is the **Justice** or **'Justice of the Peace'**. The **Magistrate** is the principal director or navigator (to steer).

He also said, **"And they will give a Mandate."** The **Mandate** is a directive or command to God's people...

This is God's Governmental realignment and the release of the **Key of the House of David** to His people - you will read more about this in coming chapters.

I will clothe him with your robe And strengthen him with your belt; I will commit your responsibility into his hand. He shall be a father to the inhabitants of Jerusalem And to the house of Judah. The key of the house of David I will lay on his shoulder; So he shall open, and no one shall shut; And he shall shut, and no one shall open. I will fasten him as a peg in a secure place, And he will become a glorious throne to his father's house. (Isaiah 22:21-23 NKJV™)

This **Changing of the Guard** will make way for the True Apostolic and Prophetic to emerge and nothing will stop it. It will come into its full fruition in 2012.

Obama Wins Presidency, Oprah Set On Fire For Jesus - She Begins Evangelism

12/30/2007

I was watching TV, and I saw (candidate) Obama and Oprah Winfrey, and she was supporting him as a candidate. At the time, the volume on the TV was all the way down and I was unsure of who he was. The Lord spoke to me and said, **"This man is the next President, he is a True Leader. I have placed Kingdom leadership in his spirit and he is the Democrat that I will 'get a hold of' of IN the White House. I have chosen him for his ability to bring UNITY to this great Nation of America and for his heart of leadership. Do not worry about what he may look like now, he will be filled and he will be set on fire for ME. He will be a praying President. People have counted him out, but I see the INNER POTENTIAL OF THIS MAN. This is the year of the UNDERDOG. Those who have been 'counted out', 'looked over' or 'thrown in the pit', I will pull them out; I will pull them up, I will bring them to the palace and they will give ALL the glory to Me because they are a humble people, a people after My own heart."**

Then the Lord said, **"Oprah will also be set on fire for ME, and she will be the greatest Evangelist that this world has ever seen - for this is her true calling and everywhere that she has been, up until this point, has been training for where I am about to take her. She influences, and has the trust of, many. I had to allow her to influence this entire generation. Soon, those who trust in her will then trust in the One True God, Jehovah."**

Fast Forward (now)

WOW!!! This was a Word that I did not want to release at the time, but it was a great test for me on 'people pleasing'. Even though my 'religious' friends ended up judging me for putting this Word out there, I had to Trust the Lord, and do what He was telling me to do. You see, at this time in my walk with God and my training in the prophetic, the Lord was 'proving' me. He was not only proving me to me, He was proving Him to me and me to others as well (although, no one should ever trust in me - only in the Lord).

There were quite a few Christians who gave me the 'dog turning its head sideways' look when I told them, "God told me Obama will be the next President..." You have to remember, this was written in December of 2007 when none of the Primaries had taken place yet...

The Lord told me that this change in Obama would come two to three years after he took office. And, I keep having a vision of Obama on his knees in the White House before an angel of the Lord. I Also see Michelle Obama as a prophet, like Deborah (Judges - Old Testament), 'Barak and Deborah'.

Well, the Lord is faithful isn't He? Yes, of course He is. Even if Obama didn't turn out to be the President, I would still trust in and serve the Lord just as passionately as I always have.

The Lord has brought me out of and through so much, that there is nothing else to do but to Love Him, Obey Him and Trust Him with my whole heart, soul, mind, will and emotions. Thank you so much Lord, for being BIG and RADICAL in my life. If we can just dare to believe Him - He will do such wonderful things in our lives. So, how about it? Will you believe with me?

GOD'S PROPHETIC ARMY IS RISING IN THE FULLNESS OF THE SPIRIT OF JOSHUA, REPOSITIONING TO A MINDSET OF UNDERSTANDING, THE WATCHMEN RISES - GO & TAKE YOUR LAND

4/21/2007, 10/31/2007, Released 10/29/2010

I felt a shift, something is breaking! A tremendous month of blessing is coming in November for those who have Persevered and Stood in the face of adversity through this year and into October. And the Lord said, **"Forget what was behind, for Victory is what you have had in this month. 'Your' October, (through the Refining by Fire) was preparing you for the Harvest. It was not only the harvest of blessing, but the harvest of souls that are soon to come. Truly, I say to you the blessing begins with this victory!"** I see the manifestation happening now and through the rest of the year. You may still be going through this test right now, but it seems to be Dissipating right before your very eyes. I hear Him saying, **"Go in and take your land!"**

And the Lord said, **"I am raising up My Prophetic Army in the fullness of Joshua and Jeremiah in the Spirit of Love. They will Stand for Truth, Justice and FREEDOM and they will not count the cost to themselves. This Army will keep advancing and continue to move forward and there will be nothing that all the power in hell and 'religion' can do to stop it! You need only but to STAND, STAND, STAND and SEE My Salvation, for the Battle is Mine, says the Lord of Hosts."**

I see the Enemy retreating, taking Leviathan, Python, Jezebel, Baal, Mammon, the Anti-Christ spirit and Rejection with him and throwing a baby fit about it (pride is immature and needs to grow up). I see a clearing for God's Love, Grace, Mercy and POWER to invade the earth. Then He said, **"The only limitation I have is your Mindset, so I AM is about to Reposition Your Mindset to that of UNDERSTANDING."** If we find ourselves feeling limited in any area, we should ask God about our mindset and He will reveal any limitation that we may have placed on ourselves and/or on Him. He said, **"There will be a Changing of the Guard. The Watchmen Prophets are Rising. The Watchmen will be the Magistrate and will give a Mandate to My people. Get ready, and Do Not be shocked when you see a Repositioning in My Body. This has to happen for My purposes to be fulfilled in the earth. Things are going to start happening OVER NIGHT and you will look and be amazed and you will say, 'Look at the HAPPENING - But only God'."**

God told Joshua to take down 'religion' and idol worship in Canaan. Jericho was the first city that was conquered in Joshua's obedience to God - this made way for the Children of Israel to go in and take the Promised Land that God had promised them. The **'walls'** of Jericho were fortified by **man's hands.** There was **great pride in their 'strength', much like the four 'walls' of man's established church system today.** There are many idols being worshiped there, and the spirit of religion is running rampant. The Lord will have no more of it. By faith and obedience of His Prophetic Army, the Walls of the established man's system church will fall. They will fall mostly because of their own Pride. When God's **Judgment & Justice** is applied to anything or anyone, the things we have sown will be reaped. *Pride goes before destruction, And a haughty spirit before a fall.* (Proverbs 16:18 NKJV™)

Scripture References

Read **Joshua Chapter 6.**

LEVIATHAN IS LURKING, THE WHEAT & THE TARES, REJOICE FOR YOUR REDEMPTION DRAWS NIGH

11/9/2007, Revised & Released 7/7/2010

Hello fellow Journeyers, Get excited because we are about to Take The Land for the Glory of our King!!! I wanted to let you know where my heart is on this one. By no means am I trying to give any glory to the enemy. I do sense from the Lord that He wants us to be aware of those things that oppose us, and be prepared with the **'tools of understanding'**, so the road ahead will be a little easier. May God bless you as you read this. I know it is a long one, but please keep reading - there is a strategy for **'Inheriting Our Land'**. I pray that as you read this Word of the Lord, you will be blessed and find **'relief'** for your souls, in Jesus Name, amen.

And the Lord said, **"Leviathan is lurking, when this one comes out, it will come out by the ROOT and the entire plant will come with it."** The **'root'** is the **love of money** - hence, the spirit of mammon. *But if it's only money these leaders are after, they'll self-destruct in no time. Lust for money brings trouble and nothing but trouble. Going down that path, some lose their footing in the faith completely and live to regret it bitterly ever after.* (1 Titus 6:9-10 *THE MESSAGE*)

And the Lord said, **"Think it not strange when there is a Shifting and Repositioning within the Body of Christ. Some of you may say, "Oh no, not another church split." I say, There is no such thing as a church split. I am refining My House, I am separating and lifting My wheat from among the tares. Those who can not withstand the fire of refining will leave. Be awake to the fact that just because some of My sheep might be leaving the 'church building', it does not mean that they are a tare, and just because they left, does not mean that they will not be back at some point. Be careful not to judge or gossip about others, this judging and gossiping will qualify you as a tare."**

"Those who are not going through the fire now have either been through it recently or will be going through it soon. Do not worry, and do not be moved to the left or to the right. I am the one who is In the intensity of this test that I have set before you for such a time as this. I am refining you to carry more of My Glory, more of My Power and more of My Presence than mankind has known on the earth before this time."

"Be Grateful. It is in this gratefulness that I will ignite the 'Law of Acceleration' and you will move quickly through this process. For I have chosen you, this generation, a people that I can trust to endure and carry this Multifaceted Mantle, for you are a Joseph generation. I have gifted you with many giftings, and it is through these giftings that My Glory will be shown in the earth. When the enemy would like to come in as a 'pack of dogs' and surround you on all fronts, he would try to attack from all angles at once, but hear what I say, he will not be able to penetrate your 'Coat of Many Colors.' It is My Three Fold anointing that I am endowing you with, a Three Fold cord that can not be broken. This anointing will break Any and All yokes of the enemy - confront him with a boldness and he will dissipate right before your very eyes. You will be as Christ was in the earth, Faith In Substance."

The Lord gave me some insight into this **Three Fold** anointing. There are three separate anointings that make up this **Three Fold** anointing that He is releasing during this season.

1. The Joseph Prophetic Anointing - from the pit to the palace, a refining must come first. Remember what Joseph had to 'go through' before he could be trusted with what God was promising him. This will bring maturity to the Body. God is **'growing us up.'** We will be a more mature, loving and understanding people. Read Genesis 37-45. Remember when Joseph flaunted his dream in front of his brothers? This was a sign of immaturity and pride on his part, ultimately casting his pearls before swine. The Lord is saying, **"Identify your pearls and do not cast them before swine."**

2. The Joshua Prophetic Anointing - the Warriors in God's unstoppable Prophetic Army, that stands for **Truth and Justice,** advancing to **'take the land'** for the glory of the Lord. He is tearing down the walls of Religion and everything that has been **'between'** us and the heart of God. Read Joshua 5:13-6:21. He is restoring the covenant of Joshua *...but as for me and my house, we will serve the LORD.* (Joshua 24:15 KJV) The Lord is restoring the **'headship'** of the true authorities in the earth and allowing them to take their rightful places of authority - **Order will be restored** (restoration of this **Order** started in 2010).

3. The Jeremiah Prophetic Anointing - the rooting out, the pulling down, destroying, and throwing down that which is not of God **and** the building up, planting on the right foundation (a foundation of perfect love), a clear vision of the cross and knowing our **True Identity In Christ**. See Jeremiah 1:10. He said that He will release the Watchmen on the wall and they will be in **"Co-ordinance"** (joint effort and destination) with the **Apostles** to set the course for the Journey ahead. See Jeremiah 31:6. This **"Co-ordinance"** is 'destination Zion' or just **Zion** (the 'Land' God has promised us, including the obedience of the body of Christ to the voice of God - **Spirit Led**). *The Scriptures provide precedent: Look! I'm setting a stone in Zion, a cornerstone in the place of honor. Whoever trusts in this stone as a foundation will never have cause to regret it. To you who trust him, he's a Stone to be proud of, but to those who refuse to trust him, The stone the workmen threw out is now the chief foundation stone. For the untrusting it's ... . a stone to trip over, a boulder blocking the way. They trip and fall because they refuse to obey* (the voice of God), *just as predicted.* (1 Peter 2:6-8 **THE MESSAGE**) More scriptures that God gave me about Zion, are at the end of this Word. **If you are an Apostle, seek God on 'partnering' with a Prophet.** They go hand in hand - there is not one without the other. I believe this is mostly for agreement, and accountability.

In addition the Lord said, **"I will release the Abrahamic Generational Blessing - the Power to get Wealth is in your midst, for true wealth is simply the absence of poverty."** True wealth has nothing to do with money or assets. True wealth is an attitude of gratitude, keeping our Focus on the Lord, and having a clear vision and Understanding of the Cross. When we come to the **understanding** that we are already **Free** then we will **Just Be Free!** Also, when we come to the **understanding** that we are already **Wealthy,** then we will **Just Be Wealthy!** He owns everything and is waiting to release it to us. The time for that release is very soon, **but our hearts have to be in the right place first.**

And the Lord said, **"Leviathan would like for you to just forget the gifts that I have entrusted you with. I choose when and who uses their giftings, not man. This spirit that wants to keep you from using your gifts is of the Anti-Christ spirit and is not to be trusted. 'Order' in a church service is one thing, but what I speak of is something else. Just as a little leaven leavens the whole lump, if something is half-truth it is still a lie. You can not compromise on this. Do not talk to, or agree with, the lying spirit. You will give it your authority if you do so. I the Lord your God will not tolerate this lying, fork tongued serpent of religion to slither among you, My people, any longer. I will drive it out by its root** (the love of mammon) **and the plant will come out with it.** (This is why there have been so many with financial troubles. The Lord is taking out the 'wrong foundation', the love of mammon. When the Lord is the foundation we will see Him as our source. When we see money as just a simple tool, then, is when we can 'have' it.) **Watch your associations. You will not want to be a part of this plant. Seek Me and I will reveal the deep things of My Spirit and of the decrement to you and you will know where I am and where I am not. Stay in Truth and more importantly in Love says the Lord of Hosts."**

The Lord gave me some things to look for regarding this Spirit. Again, not to give glory to it, but to know our enemy - this is how we know what this enemy's strategy is. Leviathan means

coiled or twisted in the Hebrew language. Where this spirit is, you will notice a lot of **chaos, noise and irritation**. It is an **enemy to the light**. There is also a sense of **false Hope** - either placing hope in wrong things or loosing hope completely. See **Job 41:9. If the hope is gone, this is a good sign that God is moving** (I will explain this later). He told me that Leviathan wants to go low, a false humility, which is actually pride in disguise. I keep seeing it slithering in basements - especially in churches where the sheep have put their hope in the building, the leadership or the ministry and **Not** in God. It is **'hiding'** so no one plainly sees it. Leviathan is the **king of the sons of pride,** see Job 41:34, **fleshy and stubborn,** and see Job 41:8. It will **sneak up from behind (accusations and back stabbing, lies, twisting the truth, puts on a Big Smoke and Lights Show)** and **hit you below the knees** (undercut your authority by convincing you that you are worthless and render you ineffective).

Spiritual authority is something that is not commonly seen, many think you need a title from man to be 'in authority' but no, God places All authority, see Romans 13:1. Spiritual authority is mostly unseen and it **Just Is**, like an evangelist who does not refer to himself as one, but is just that, an evangelist. This is why we should not fear what man can do to us - they cannot take away what God Himself has established.

Like I said before, Leviathan likes to sneak up from behind and hit us below the knees, so we don't see what hit us. It tries to get us to resolve what we think happened (easy to not link it back to the spirit realm), by looking at other people as the problem (it hides behind other things and is very cowardly). You may think you are dealing with just a 'lying spirit' or a 'spirit of pride' when in fact it is something else (the root here is the **love of mammon**). Leviathan also uses many **diversions to distract** and it tries to get us to **'change the subject'** instead of answering a question directly and honestly. **Fear is behind the lie.** It tries to get us to **steal the credit for accomplishments** that are not ours. It 'gets us in debt' too - it tries to get us to reward ourselves with 'a false blessing.' This is the same as **getting ahead of God** (which is not good). This is **spiritual Pride.** It attempts to stop deliverance because it has a heart that is **'hard as stone.'** See Job 41:24. It attracts **thievery and a gypsy lifestyle to us** - moving from one place to another because the newness of something is 'exciting' but when the 'newness' wears off, or we 'figure it's lies out', it flees the scene - **there is usually a lot of shame involved**. We will see traits like these manifest from people as this thing leaves them. Also, the **'lack' of money**, in most cases, is a **'trigger'** for Leviathan to manifest. This is the main reason why our harvest has been held up. The Lord is going to take care of this thing Himself, and release the harvest to us. *In that day the Lord, with his great and strong and cruel sword, will send punishment on Leviathan, the quick-moving snake, and on Leviathan, the twisted snake; and he will put to death the dragon which is in the sea.* (Isaiah 27:1 BBE)

There is also a **'false responsibility'** with this spirit - it wants you to come into covenant with it by having sympathy for it, it will **speak seductive words and in turn ask you to take responsibility for it's wrong actions** almost like an enabler would. See Job 41:3-4. Always remember to **separate the person from the spirit** and **show the person love and understanding and Give Mercy and Grace. Do not confront this thing,** you will regret it. See Job 41:8. **The Lord told me it is His battle.** Keep quiet and **do not let it know you are on to it.** God just wants us to Love people, kind of like an addict coming off of a drug - show them love and comfort, you are their link to God until they can turn to Him themselves as the pride leaves. The pride will leave because of the Christ-like Love that you Give. Someone has got to give and this is what will break pride and allow for people to be restored. A **'deliverance session' is not going to work with this one, this is God's battle.** *And Jehovah said to me, You have seen well; for I will watch over My Word to perform it.* (Jeremiah 1:12 MKJV)

I keep seeing God's hand grasping a bundle of wheat and uprooting it. Within this wheat there are tares, and He is separating the wheat from the tares. He is putting the wheat into the barn and the tares are being burned in the fire (this is the refiner's fire). He said, **"What is left is as purified gold and this is the Rock in which I will build MY church on - the church without spot or wrinkle. It is this Unmovable, Unshakable foundation that I can then build Love, Truth and Light on. Then the harvest will come, then the harvest will come. Do not be moved, do not be moved for your redemption draws nigh, says the Lord of Hosts."**

God will always do what is right and best for us - because it can be a painful process, we can sometimes see it as something bad. Let me assure you, He is FOR US, and He is ultimately thinking of our future and our wholeness. He has His hand on us and is always working ALL things out for our good. The beauty that will come out of these painful times is **Destiny Fulfilled.** It is what we were created to, do, and be, IN HIM. This is where we will ultimately be the happiest.

The scripture below is depicting the emerging of His Kingdom here on Earth. I saw a parallel to this scripture and what God is doing right now In Us. *So shall it be at the end of the world: the angels shall come forth, and sever the wicked from among the just, And shall cast them into the furnace of fire: there shall be wailing and gnashing of teeth.* (Matthew 13:49-50 KJV) The angels are being sent to bring deliverance to all of mankind, for the purging of our hearts, and removing that which is not of God - the tares. We are going through this Fire right now and let me tell you, there is a lot of wailing and gnashing of teeth happening all around. All of mankind is manifesting ugly things as 'the tares' are on their way out. If things seem scary, do not worry, it is temporary and your redemption draws nigh. The reason that it hurts so much when these things are taken from us, is because we have had some level of hope in them (a false comfort), **we have had our focus on them and our foundation has been built on them - false hope**. And the Lord sad, **"Come boldly to the thrown of Grace and ask what you will for now is the season for unusual favor, go towards what opposes you, see it dissipate, go in and**

Take Your Land!!! Says the Lord of Hosts." *Let us therefore come boldly to the throne of grace, that we may obtain mercy, and find grace to help in time of need.* (Hebrews 4:16 KJV) *...he that putteth his Trust in me shall possess the land, and shall inherit my holy mountain;* (Isaiah 57:13 KJV)

So, to recap, do not worry, the thing that tries to make you fear is a smoke screen, it deceives - keep moving forward - the reason there is such an uproar is because **we are on the right path and the enemy is freaking out!** Keep moving forward - what is causing fear will dissipate right before your eyes. God is ripping the wrong foundation out of our hearts. These things have been so deep-seated that we cannot even see them and most are generational. This is causing us to 'feel' Hopeless for a short time, until we see our need for **repentance**, and **turn our complete Trust to God alone as our source.** You see, up until now, we have found our Identity in false hope, wrong foundation and our accomplishments (or lack of accomplishments). Those things can and will fail and disappoint us.

When we turn to Him - **He will Give us a Heart Understanding of what our true Identity is - who we are IN Christ, the Hope of Glory in the earth**. That way, when the 'things' fail us, we will not be destroyed because our identity will be in the One who is infallible. Then I heard God say, **"Then the harvest can come, then the harvest can come."** *Do not let your heart envy sinners; but be in the fear of Jehovah all the day long. For surely there is a hereafter, and your Hope shall not be cut off.* (Proverbs 23:17-18 MKJV)

The Lord showed me that if we were to reap the harvest with the wrong foundation in our heart it would destroy us. Money is a magnifier to what is already in a person's heart. If He alone is the foundation in our hearts, when the money is applied it will glorify Him.

44

Here is the Strategy for this season:

1. Watch your associations. Identify your pearls and do not cast them before swine.

2. Do not talk to or agree with the lying spirit. You give it your authority when you do. Do not agree with the lying spirit - say something like, "I'm sorry to hear you feel that way."

3. Do not confront this spirit (or its many heads). The Lord showed us it is His battle. Keep quiet and do not let it know you are on to it.

4. Stay in Truth and more importantly in Love.

5. If you are an Apostle, seek God on 'partnering' with a Prophet. They go hand in hand - there is not one without the other.

6. Seek Him and He will reveal the deep things of His Spirit and of the decrement to you and you will know where He is and where He is not.

7. Remember that the 'lack' of money in most cases is a 'trigger' for Leviathan to manifest - you will know it when you see it.

8. Separate the person from the spirit, show the person love and understanding and Give Mercy and Grace. God just wants us to Love people, like an addict coming off of a drug - show them love and comfort, you are their link to God until they can turn to Him themselves as the pride leaves. The pride will leave because of the Christ-like Love that you Give. Someone has got to give and this is what will break pride and allow for people to be restored. Love breaks the back of pride and allows a door to be open for the Lord to get in.

Scripture References

Read Exodus 12:1-39, 1 Corinthians 5 and Matthew 13:18-58.

Be glad then, sons of Zion, and rejoice in Jehovah your God. For He has given you the former rain according to righteousness, and He will cause the rain to come down for you, the former rain and the latter rain in the first month. And the floors shall be full of wheat, and the vats shall overflow with wine and oil. And I will restore to you the years which the swarming locust has eaten, the locust larvae, and the stripping locust, and the cutting locust, My great army which I sent among you. And you shall eat in plenty, and be satisfied, and praise the name of Jehovah your God, who has dealt with you wonderfully; and My people shall never be ashamed. And you shall know that I am in the midst of Israel, and that I am Jehovah your God, and no one else; and My people shall never be ashamed. And it shall be afterward, I will pour out My Spirit on all flesh. And your sons and your daughters shall prophesy; your old men shall dream dreams; your young men shall see visions. (Joel 2:23-28 MKJV)

In a recent Word I released, God said, **"There will be a Great Awakening - Wake Up, Wake Up, Wake Up!"**

Awake! Awake! Put on your strength, Zion; put on your beautiful robes, O Jerusalem, the holy city. For never again shall come to you uncircumcised and unclean ones. Shake yourself from the dust; rise up! Sit, Jerusalem! Free yourself from your neckbands, O captive daughter of Zion. For so says Jehovah, You were sold for nothing; and you shall not be redeemed with silver. For so says the Lord Jehovah, My people went down before into Egypt to stay there; and the Assyrian oppressed them without cause. Now therefore, what have I here, says Jehovah, that My people are taken away for nothing? Those who rule make them howl, says Jehovah; and without ceasing My name is blasphemed every day. Therefore My people shall know My name; So it shall be in that day, for I am He who speaks; behold, it is I. How beautiful on the mountains are the feet of him who brings good tidings, making peace heard; who brings good news, making salvation heard; who says to Zion, Your God reigns! The voice of Your watchmen shall lift up! They lift up the voice together; they sing aloud. For they shall see eye to eye, when Jehovah shall bring again Zion. Break out, sing together, waste places of Jerusalem; for Jehovah has comforted His people; He has redeemed Jerusalem. Jehovah has bared His holy arm in the eyes of all the nations; and all the ends of the earth shall see the salvation of our God. Turn! Turn! Go out from there! Touch not the unclean. Go out of her midst; purify yourself, bearers of the vessels of Jehovah. For you shall not go out with haste, nor go by flight; for Jehovah will go before you; and the God of Israel gathers you. (Isaiah 52:1-12 MKJV)

So they shall fear the name of Jehovah from the west, and His glory from the rising of the sun. When the enemy shall come in like a flood, the Spirit of Jehovah shall make him flee. And the Redeemer shall come to Zion, and to those who turn from transgression in Jacob, says Jehovah. As for Me, this is My covenant with them, says Jehovah; My Spirit that is on you, and My Words which I have put in your mouth, shall not depart out of your mouth, nor out of the mouth of your seed, nor out of the mouth of your seed's seed, says Jehovah, from now on and forever. (Isaiah 59:19-21 MKJV)

Therefore they shall come and sing in the height of Zion, Streaming to the goodness of the Lord - For wheat and new wine and oil, For the young of the flock and the herd; Their souls shall be like a well-watered garden, And they shall sorrow no more at all. (Jeremiah 31:12 NKJV™)

POLARITY - I AM, IS BRINGING ALL THINGS INTO ALIGNMENT, THIS IS A NOW WORD

1/16/2008, Revised & Released 8/6/2010

My husband, Chad, was telling me once that there was going to be a full moon, he said that was significant in some way, but he didn't know how yet. Then later, we were riding in the car and I looked up at the full moon, and I heard God say just one word, **"Polarity."** The definition of Polarity is (think of this in spiritual terms - pertaining to the Body of Christ) - that quality of a body in virtue of which peculiar properties reside in certain points; usually, as in electrified or magnetized bodies, properties of attraction or repulsion, or the power of taking a certain direction. Thus we speak of the polarity of the magnet or magnetic needle, whose pole is not always that of the earth, but a point somewhat easterly or westerly; and the deviation of the needle from a north and south line is called its variation (Sphere of Influence). A mineral is said to possess polarity, when it attracts one pole of a magnetic needle and repels the other. Magnetism - Power of attraction; as the magnetism of interest Magnetize - To communicate magnetic properties to any thing; as, to magnetize a needle. Magnetizing - Imparting magnetism to. The magnet is said to be able to cure diseases.

Then God said, **"Polarity equals True Repentance - Returning to the Top equals Right Relationship and Right Standing with Me and True Headship restored in the earth realm. By My GRACE I will realign ALL things."** The planets are coming into alignment too. He then said, **"I am bringing all things into alignment, or position, to receive the POWER that I am about to impart to My people. These are my Josephs, a remnant of people in which I am well pleased. I have hidden you away for such a time as this. My precious ones, who love ME so much, the thought of sinning does not even enter into their minds. Just as Joseph found favor with the prison guard, I am about to 'Magnetize' My people and they will become 'attractive' to ALL types of people around them. They will HAVE favor in** the most unlikely places and with the most unlikely people, for a season of Miracles is upon you. **You will see an outpouring of My Spirit and many will be saved and many will be healed for My Namesake and My Glory. Kingdom and 'Kingdom Business' will be the order of the day; not only in the hearts and the minds of the Body of Christ, but also with those of the 'world'** - these people are My 'future' people and since, where I AM there is no space or time, they ARE My people because everything belongs to ME, says God. **You will see these Kingdom workers coming out of nowhere and many will say, "Where have they come from?" They will have TRUE leadership in their hearts. No, no man has taught them this kind or type of leadership, for these are the true, chosen leaders of this generation. These leaders that that I have chosen did not have to be taught by books or by man, but by My Spirit. They will be a fierce Prophetic Army with the heart of Joshua** - **they will have My directive; a passionate people, violent and passionate in LOVE. They will take the Kingdom and they will take it by force. Just as I have positioned them to receive the blessing I have also positioned them in hiding, so they may ambush their enemy when it is least expected and they will see their enemy's power dissipate before their very eyes. You have only, but to STAND and not move, and you will see your enemies become your footstool, says the Lord of Hosts."** Our enemies are the spirits, not the people - we need to respect and love people and separate them from what may be driving them.

He then said, **"It's been a long and hard wilderness, many have been hurting - old betrayals and habits have come back to haunt you in this past season. I have caused a 'forced rest' of sorts for many of you, especially My Apostles and My Prophets** (some of you do not know that you are Apostles or Prophets yet). **I have chosen this down time for you - to first of all find rest, but also to center down, or become present and to finally forgive old hurts from the past that have either plagued you or you have forgotten about. I also needed to fine tune your hearing so I could speak to you, allow you to learn of ME, to get a revelation of the strategy for what is to come and to** show you some things that you have over looked because of the business of life and the pursuit of mammon. I will change the direction in which your focus has taken you and put it back on Me. I need you to lead this next generation in the right direction. Your question is not to ask WHY are these seemingly negative things happening to me, but to ask WHAT? What is it you are trying to get to me Lord? I will download you with the correct 'co-ordinance' very soon." (This 'Co-Ordinance' He is talking about is Zion the Holy Mountain. He said that the Apostles and the Prophets would be in a 'partnership' of sorts, a trust, for agreement and accountability.) **"You have but to keep your eyes on Me and Trust Me. Do not worry, things will get better soon. I have My hand on these situations all around you. Several of you have had issues with your spine - this is directly parallel to the alignment that is taking place in the spirit realm on your behalf and in others around you. When something is out of place for a long time it can feel normal, comfortable or even good to you, but when it finally gets put back into alignment it can be painful and take a little time to adjust to the new positioning. Just as a plant that is uprooted and planted in a different place can 'feel shock' so have you felt the shock of this realignment."**

Recently my dear husband Chad, gave me a hydrangea bush for Mother's Day. It had very beautiful violet colored flowers and it was a very healthy looking plant. He lovingly re-potted it for me in a much larger pot and used a different type of soil, different than it was first planted in. A few days later it began to wilt, even though I had watered and cared for it. The flowers began to change colors - to a blue and pinkish color (these colors were even more beautiful to me). I searched online and found that the hydrangea will change colors if you put it in different types of soil and the plant may 'feel shock' and droop for a while until the root system gets used to the new soil. The Lord showed me that this is an example of how we may 'feel shock' for a while until we have changed our direction and are **rooted and grounded on the ROCK,** Him of course, as our foundation. The foundation we have been used to is mammon, or the love of money. Yes, it has been in most everyone's hearts, at such a deep level, that we couldn't see it before now. Do not feel bad - just be glad that God is doing this **'heart work'** in us on our behalf.

And then He said, **"Remember, you battle not against flesh and blood, but against principalities, some in particular, Leviathan, Python, Jezebel, Baal, Rejection, Anti-Christ and Mammon. They have been working together in the earth for generations to try and bind My people into a stagnate existence - into a 'Children of Israel Mentality.' I AM is lifting these foul, dark generals from My people and the separation causes great pain and 'gnashing of teeth.' They have been the very foundation and support for so many, for generations, but I will have it no more. This spiritual uprooting can manifest as pain in the physical realm. Many of you have had a realignment in your very spines as a result, do not worry, this is a good thing for you, this will bring Health and Life back to your physical bodies as well."**

All of the recent earthquakes are a sign in the earth that the spirit realm is being 'shaken up', and so are the hearts, minds and psyche of people all over the world. And the Lord said, **"Do not worry my children, you can say, "All is well with my soul." And, keep telling yourself that, until you believe it. This is a time of stripping away the things that were Not necessary, especially religious mindsets, and what is underneath, can sometimes be foul. It is this revelation of truth that will jolt your soul into a wanting to be righteous and a need for repentance. I am taking you from a 'head knowledge of Me' to a 'Heart Understanding' of who I AM is. You will HAVE the Understanding of what it means to be 'IN CHRIST -The Hope of Glory in the Earth.' This process is different for everyone and will take different amounts of time for everyone. Remember to stay In Love and also remember to ask, 'WHAT is it that you are trying to get to me Lord?' instead of, 'WHY am I going through this?' This 'shaking' will reveal the 'False Apostolic spirit' that exists now in the earth and spur on changes for the better in all areas of your life. When your FOCUS is turned to Me you will start to see finances loosened** up and blessing on your finances and businesses. Dreams that you have waited and waited for, waited to come to pass for a very long time, and in-fact had given up on, will come into manifestation Overnight. These dreams had to fall to the ground and die first before I could resurrect them, in My timing, the time when you are mature enough to have them come to pass without them destroying you and without them making you turn away from Me. Remember, money is a magnifier to what is already in a person's heart, if I had given you the money before your heart was in the right place it would destroy you. You will have unheard of favor this year. Put to use the scraps of those things that you once had hope for, the things that you could find no practical application for at the time, but I will show you now how they can be useful, to put to use and become 'Substance.' Look and ascend up to where your help comes from, for it comes from the Lord. Rejoice for The Spirit of FREEDOM is in your midst and redemption draws nigh says the Lord of Hosts."

Scripture References

A Song of Degrees. I will lift up my eyes to the hills. Where shall my help come from? My help comes from Jehovah, who made Heaven and earth. He will not allow you foot to be moved; He who keeps you will not slumber. Behold, He who keeps Israel shall neither slumber nor sleep. Jehovah is your keeper; Jehovah is your shade on your right hand. The sun shall not strike you by day, nor the moon by night. Jehovah shall keep you from all evil; He shall keep your soul. Jehovah shall keep your going out and your coming in from this time forth, and even forevermore. (Psalms 121:1-8 MKJV)

And from the days of John the Baptist until now the kingdom of heaven suffers violence, and the violent take it by force. For all the prophets and the law prophesied until John. And if you are willing to receive it, he is Elijah who is to come. He who has ears to hear, let him hear! "But to what shall I liken this generation? It is like children sitting in the marketplaces and calling to their companions, and saying: 'We played the flute for you, And you did not dance; We mourned to you, And you did not lament.' For John came neither eating nor drinking, and they say, 'He has a demon.' The Son of Man came eating and drinking, and they say, 'Look, a glutton and a winebibber, a friend of tax collectors and sinners!' But wisdom is justified by her children." Then He began to rebuke the cities in which most of His mighty works had been done, because they did not repent: (Matthew 11:12-20 NKJV™)

All things are delivered to Me by My Father. And no one knows the Son except the Father. Nor does anyone know the Father except the Son, and the one to whom the Son will reveal Him. Come to Me all you who labor and are heavy laden, and I will give you rest. Take My yoke on you and learn of Me, for I am meek and lowly in heart, and you shall find rest to your souls. For My yoke is easy, and My burden is light. (Matthew 11:27-30 MKJV)

And I will bring the blind by a way that they knew not; I will lead them in paths (roads) *that they have not known: I will make darkness light before them, and crooked things* (ways) *straight. These things will I do unto them, and not forsake them.* (Isaiah 42:16 KJV)

But the LORD was with Joseph and showed him mercy, and He gave him favor in the sight of the keeper of the prison. (Genesis 39:21 NKJV™)

If my people, which are called by my name, shall humble themselves, and pray, and seek my face, and turn from their wicked ways; then will I hear from heaven, and will forgive their sin, and will heal their land. Now mine eyes shall be open, and mine ears attent unto the prayer that is made in this place. For now have I chosen and sanctified this house, that my name may be there for ever: and mine eyes and mine heart shall be there perpetually. And as for thee, if thou wilt walk before me, as David thy father walked, and do according to all that I have commanded thee, and shalt observe my statutes and my judgments; Then will I stablish the throne of thy kingdom, according as I have covenanted with David thy father, saying, There shall not fail thee a man to be ruler in Israel. (2 Chronicles 7:14-18 KJV)

Likewise reckon ye also yourselves to be dead indeed unto sin, but alive unto God through Jesus Christ our Lord. Let not sin therefore reign in your mortal body, that ye should obey it in the lusts thereof. Neither yield ye your members as instruments of unrighteousness unto sin: but yield yourselves unto God, as those that are alive from the dead, and your members as instruments of righteousness unto God. For sin shall not have dominion over you: for ye are not under the law, but under grace. What then? shall we sin, because we are not under the law, but under grace? God forbid. (Romans 6:11-15 KJV)

A Psalm of David. The LORD said unto my Lord, Sit thou at my right hand, until I make thine enemies thy footstool. (Psalms 110:1 KJV)

"JUST BE - STEP INTO THE FLOW OF MY SPIRIT, I WILL LAUNCH YOU INTO YOUR DESTINY"

1/16/2008, Revised & Released 5/12/2010

At a gathering a Pastor friend of mine said, **"Just Be"** to me. I didn't really understand what she was telling me at the time, but the Lord began revealing it to me and this is what He told me.

Many of us have gone through one test after another, one trial after another and one sickness after another, and God said, **"This will subside, and you will step into My Glory, into My Power, and into a place where you will not have to 'Enter In' to my Spirit because you will already be there. This IS being Present in the moment. Not living in the past or the future but Being in the NOW where My Peace lives - the very definition of FAITH. Your Spiritual Gifts are the KEY to unlock my Power such as the world has never seen. There will be no more 'One Man Show', there will be no more 'Business As Usual', there will be no more 'Status Quo', there will be no more 'Mediocrity', there will be no more 'Good Ol' Boys'. These are all of the spirit of COMPETITION & COMPROMISE which is a spirit that is in league with the spirit of DECEIT and THE PRIDE OF MAN. This power that you may see is NOT My true power. These are false and are the imitation of the One True Power - My Grace. The Days of the Powerless House of God are over!!! I am evicting these foul ego-driven spirits from My temple. My Spirit is that of LOVE and Compassion and not of Man and Wrong Judgment. The false Apostolic will be exposed and will step aside for the True Apostolic to emerge."**

The Lord then showed me that He created us with our giftings, just as He intertwined our feelings and emotions in us for use, so are the giftings that God has chosen to use through us. And the Lord said, **"This part of so many of My people has been lying dormant, so much so, that they do not even think that they are gifted at all. I have given these diverse gifts to ALL men, and I will jump start these gifts as the shift of this New Year takes**

place. (Remember a prophetic Word is for the time when it is received - there is no time or space in the spirit realm.) **Those who have been fasting, sowing and obeying My Voice, and those who are LOVE motivated, will see a shift, a jump-start and a launching into My Anointing, Grace, Ability and Power. You will see manifestation in you and all around you. Just as an electric shock will restart a heart, so will I 'reprogram' and 'restart' your heart, and you will have a new heart, My heart. You will know what My heart is and you will be able to navigate easily because it will not be your heart leading you, but you will have My heart in you, leading and guiding you, says the Lord of Hosts."**

Above, where God talks about **fasting, sowing, obedience and love motivation** - these are strategies in the spirit. They are laws that bring cause and effect into our physical realm. **Fasting** cleanses our vessels (bodies) and allows us to forsake the flesh. This in turn allows us to hear God's voice very clearly. He gives us understanding that we previously didn't have - answers come when we fast. It also gives us access to authority to overcome certain spirits - read in the Bible where Jesus said, *"These come out but by prayer and fasting."* He was talking about the spirit of Unbelief and deaf and dumb spirits. **Sowing** gives God legal authority to 'give' something back to you. God is not mocked, that which a man sows, he shall also reap. If you have been reaping negative things, take a look at your sowing. Even the very energy and thoughts we project, is a form of sowing. This is why the Bible says to take every thought captive unto the obedience of Christ. **Obedience** brings God's favor, and when it is an **obedience of sacrifice** it will bring the Generational blessing of Abraham. We have to have a **Love Motivation**, you see, we cannot fool God, He knows and sees ALL things and what He looks at, is our **Hearts Intent**. Our hearts intent is hidden, even from us, most of the time, especially when we are in something for our own glory or wanting to have praise from others. If we need praise or approval from others, then we are in pride and God simply moves on and comes back when we 'grow up' and are ready to Love and Give Unconditionally with no thought of ourselves or any thought of reward. Remember this verse… *Likewise, younger ones, be subject to older ones, and all being subject to one another.* **Put on humility. For God resists proud ones, but He gives grace** (His Power) **to the humble.** (1 Peter 5:5 MKJV)

And the Lord said, **"The use of your gifts brings more flow. This is the KEY to the flow. If you are given something you must give it away to receive more. To keep the flow flowing, you must give what you have away. If you do not use your gifts, I can not give you any further provision for your vision. Do not block up the flow, so jump in, for there is coming a Great Awakening, a Great Awakening - WAKE UP, WAKE UP, WAKE UP!!! Step into the FLOW and Just BE in it - No Bones - just flow. Just FLOW and BE who I have created you to be, Says the Lord of Hosts."**

No Bones means to be forthright and candid about; acknowledge freely, no excuses and with **no FEAR**. When we minister, and pride or fear is attached in any way, it becomes perverted and that is not a good place to be. This is what makes a false prophet. I hear the Lord saying, **"Come Boldly to My thrown of Grace and ask what you will."** Boldly, but Humbly…

God showed me that ministering in pride and fear is one of the reasons the church today has a Poverty or **'Children of Israel'** Mentality (when it comes to the Kingdom and their Giftings). We need to stop being in fear about using our gifts - God gave them to us for us to use them. He said to me, **"Would you give someone a car and expect them to just park it in the driveway just to say that they had it, but they could never drive it?"** Of course not, it is the same with everything that God has given us. It is to be used to **GLORIFY THE KING OF GLORY**. He also said, **"When people step into this flow and start just flowing in and with the gifts that I have created inside of them, this is where 'THEIR MONEY IS' - their provision. The wealth transfer is in this obedience."** Remember, **MONEY IS JUST A TOOL**, it is not our source.

Order, Respect, and Respect for Authority are some very important keys to live by...

Order & Respect - we must stay **In Order** where ever we may be. If we are at a church that does not allow their members to use their gifts, we **must** respect that. We then use our gifts where we can. Be sure the authority is okay with it. If we step out without the authorities blessing we **will not be** ministering by the Spirit of the Lord. As we use our gifts, we will learn and grow and **MATURE IN CHRIST** - this is the Hope of Glory in the Earth. Many ministries do not want a lot of people just using their gifts haphazardly, because many are not mature yet. When pride is present, the gifts end up getting used in error.

What is it that makes us 'mature in Christ?' I will discuss this later in the Word called, **"THE GREAT AWAKENING HAS COME, THE VEIL OF RELIGION IS BEING LIFTED, "I AM WILL CLEAN YOUR HANDS AND RENEW YOUR MIND, REJOICE FOR YOUR REDEMPTION DRAWS NIGH" SALVATION IS HERE & NOW, WE ARE FREE."**

Respect for Authority is **very important.** If we are disrespecting our authority, we cannot expect anything to get from God to us. When we are not respecting all other people, we 'put a kink' in the garden hose, so to speak. The anointing flows from the top down and if there is a kink in the hose, nothing will get to us. This is also an area of pride and God does what? He resists the proud and gives grace to the Humble... Also, the Bible tells us to respect our authorities, if we do not, we are 'out of order' and God cannot legally bless us not just in ministry, but in all of life. This includes our President. I know many have been indignant over many different things regarding our President and his policies. We can dislike the policies and even the way the man does things, and still respect the office and separate the person from the spirit that may be behind some policies. We are not here to control others, we are here to love and pray for others. When we attack those that we think are in error, we are in error.

Please stop speaking against the President!

Our words are powerful and when we talk about what he is doing or the way he believes, we just keep him trapped in a cycle. If we, as the people of God, would respect our authority, the President, and pray for him and speak positive things about him (you know, speak those things that are not as though they were, Romans 4:17 paraphrased), then God can step in and change things. This is part of the power that God gave to us in the earth. When we disrespect authority we are putting ourselves in **direct opposition to God** and going against what He Himself has done (read Romans 13:1-2), and in turn directly oppose God.

With regards to **Respect for Authority, Please, Do Not** let the enemy win this one! He has repeatedly fooled a lot of Christians into thinking that they are 'doing God a favor', when in fact, they are just bringing judgment on themselves and the body of Christ. Remember, Satan was 'Lucifer' - a beautiful angel that was created by God to 'minister' to God. He wound up disrespecting his authority, God, and he was thrown out of Heaven. God looks over His Word to perform it. He has to abide by His own Word or it would make Him a liar. God is NOT a liar. Anytime we get our Focus off of the Lord, in anything, we are IN PRIDE. This is what Lucifer did. He changed his focus to himself instead of God - and God, in turn, had to 'resist' Him. Please do not fall into this trap. Let's all keep our Focus on God and not on what others may or may not be doing. Then God will bring Justice to the situation.

The Lord gave me a vision of this **FLOW** and He said, **"It is like a river that is flowing and some of My people have already jumped in with their whole heart, their whole soul, their whole mind and all of their strength, but others have made camp in the World on the shore of My great river, where they think it is safe because it 'looks' safe to them - they are not discerning rightly. THE ONLY PLACE WHERE IT IS SAFE IS**

IN MY FLOW. Stepping into My flow and using the gifts that I have created in you, will bring MY GLORY on the earth - this is what My Kingdom on the earth is. It originates inside of you, and wants to be let out. This IS seeking Me and My Kingdom first. If you seek Me and My Kingdom first ALL the things that you think you have to 'get' for yourself, will simply be added with no struggle and no burden on your shoulders. Take a chance on Me and Jump into My Flow, and it will take you to your True Destiny, your True Purpose, for this is a season of Destiny and a season of Purpose and a season of Dreams becoming a reality. I need you to truly put Me first and step out into My Flow says The Lord of Hosts."

Scripture References

Read Matthew 6:19-34.

Obey the rulers who have authority over you. **Only God can give authority to anyone, and he puts these rulers in their places of power. People who oppose the authorities are opposing what God has done,** *and they will be punished.* (Romans 13:1-2 CEV)

And it will come about, in the last days, says God, that **I will send out my Spirit on all flesh;** *and your sons and your daughters will be prophets, and your young men will see visions, and your old men will have dreams: And on my men-servants and my women-servants I will send my Spirit, and they will be prophets.* (Acts 2:17-18 BBE)

Now concerning spiritual gifts, brethren, I would not have you ignorant. Ye know that ye were Gentiles, carried away unto these dumb idols, even as ye were led. Wherefore I give you to understand, that no man speaking by the Spirit of God calleth Jesus accursed: and that no man can say that Jesus is the Lord, but by the Holy Ghost. (A true prophet calls Jesus Lord - a false prophet speaks against Jesus or doesn't call Jesus Lord.) *Now there are diversities of gifts, but the same Spirit. And there are differences of administrations, but the same Lord. And there are diversities of operations, but it is the same God which worketh all in all. But the manifestation of the Spirit is given to every man to profit withal.* (Our gifts are given for the purpose of edifying the body of Christ and to bring others to the saving knowledge of Jesus.) *For to one is given by the Spirit the word of wisdom; to another the word of knowledge by the same Spirit; To another faith by the same Spirit; to another the gifts of healing by the same Spirit; To another the working of miracles; to another prophecy; to another discerning of spirits; to another divers kinds of tongues; to another the interpretation of tongues: But all these worketh that one and the selfsame Spirit, dividing to every man severally as He will.* (God uses who He chooses to use and uses what gift through whomever He chooses - it is up to Him.) *For as the body is one, and hath many members, and all the members of that one body, being many, are one body: so also is Christ. For by one Spirit are we all baptized into one body, whether we be Jews or Gentiles, whether we be bond or free; and have been all made to drink into one Spirit. For the body is not one member, but many. If the foot shall say, Because I am not the hand, I am not of the body; is it therefore not of the body? And if the ear shall say, Because I am not the eye, I am not of the body; is it therefore not of the body? If the whole body were an eye, where were the hearing? If the whole were hearing, where were the smelling? But now hath God set the members every one of them in the body, as it hath pleased Him. And if they were all one member, where were the body? But now are they many members, yet but one body. And the eye cannot say unto the hand, I have no need of thee: nor again the head to the feet, I have no need of you. Nay, much more those members of the body, which seem to be more feeble, are necessary: And those members of the body, which we think to be less honourable, upon these we bestow more abundant honor; and our uncomely parts have more abundant comeliness. For our comely parts have no need: but God hath tempered the body together, having given more abundant honor to that part which lacked: That there should be no schism* (division in religious denomination) *in the body; but that the members should have the same care one for another. And whether one member suffer, all the members suffer with it; or one member be honoured, all the members rejoice with it.* (He is telling us that there should be no jealousy or competition among the people in the Body.) *Now ye are the body of Christ, and members in particular. And God hath set some in the church, first apostles, secondarily prophets, thirdly teachers, after that miracles, then gifts of healings, helps, governments, diversities of tongues. Are all apostles? are all prophets? are all teachers? are all workers of miracles? Have all the gifts of healing? do all speak with tongues? do all interpret? But covet earnestly the best gifts: and yet shew I unto you a more excellent way.* (1 Corinthians 12:1-31 KJV)

The above chapter of scripture is not meant as an instruction to compete. What God is saying here, is for us to desire to have the **'best gifts'** so you will be able to hear from Him easily and see what is ahead of you. It is an important asset for us to have Apostolic and Prophetic understanding and vision. If He is saying here to covet earnestly these gifts that means that He is making them accessible to **all of us.** For God to be **able to trust you,** the real question is, are you willing to **'GO THROUGH' to obtain a maturity** with these gifts? Also, just because there may be several people in a church with a 'prophetic gift' doesn't mean that there cannot be more. We need to open our minds to many or rather, **all** possibilities - we serve a very Big God!

*And thou shall **love the Lord thy God** with all thy heart, and with all thy soul, and with all thy mind, and with all thy strength: this is the first commandment. And the second is like, namely this, Thou shall **love thy neighbor as thyself.** There is none other commandment greater than these.* (Mark 12:30-31 KJV)

*But **seek ye first the Kingdom of God,** and his righteousness; and all these things shall be added unto you.* (Matthew 6:33 KJV)

*But if I **cast out devils by the Spirit of God,** then the kingdom of God is come unto you.* (Matthew 12:28 KJV)

*And he said, Unto you **it is given to know the mysteries of the kingdom of God:** but to others in parables; that seeing they might not see, and hearing they might not understand.* (Luke 8:10 KJV)

And heal the sick that are therein, and say unto them, The kingdom of God is come nigh unto you. (Luke 10:9 KJV)

But if I with the finger of God cast out devils, no doubt the kingdom of God is come upon you. (Luke 11:20 KJV)

Neither shall they say, Lo here! or, lo there! for, behold, the kingdom of God is within you. (Luke 17:21 KJV)

Do not be deceived, God is not mocked. For whatever a man sows, that he also will reap. For he sowing to his flesh will reap corruption from the flesh. But he sowing to the Spirit will reap life everlasting from the Spirit. But we should not lose heart in well-doing, for in due season we shall reap, if we do not faint. (Galatians 6:7-9 MKJV)

And seeing that a crowd is running together, Jesus rebuked the unclean spirit, saying to him, **Dumb and deaf** *spirit, I command you, come out of him and enter no more into him! And the spirit cried out, throwing him into convulsions, and came out of him. And he was like one dead, so that many said, He is dead. But Jesus took him by the hand and lifted him up, and he arose. And He entering into a house, His disciples asked Him privately, Why could we not cast him out? And He said to them,* **This kind can come out by nothing except by prayer and fasting.** (Mark 9:25-29 MKJV)

For the weapons of our warfare are not fleshly, but mighty through God to the pulling down of strongholds, pulling down imaginations and every high thing that exalts itself against the knowledge of God, and bringing into **captivity every thought into the obedience of Christ;** *and having readiness to avenge all disobedience, when your obedience is fulfilled.* (2 Corinthians 10:4-6 MKJV)

Since then we have a great High Priest who has passed into the heavens, Jesus the Son of God, let us hold fast our profession. For we do not have a high priest who cannot be touched with the feelings of our infirmities, but was in all points tempted just as we are, yet without sin. Therefore **let us come boldly to the throne of grace, that we**

may obtain mercy and find grace to help in time of need.
(Hebrews 4:14-16 MKJV)

Kings & Priests, Kingdom Marketplace & Giftings

1/17/2008

The Lord gave me a revelation regarding Kings and Priests. Yes, the Kings are supposed to be in the marketplace and ministering there and helping the Priests be the Priests, but scripture in the book of Revelation tells us that He has made us **Kings and Priests.** He has made us **both** Kings and Priests. Not just a King or just a Priest. Therefore, the Lord showed me, the Kings must be Kingly, but have a Kingdom/Priestly mindset, and the Priests must be Priestly, but have a Kingdom/Kingly mindset. Therefore, the **Priests must also be thinking Kingdom in the giving arena.** Priests are **not exempt from giving.** This is where many in 'man's church system' have gotten into the poverty mindset. Many, not all, but many of the Priests have thought that they are receivers only, but this is not true. They are to be just as much a part of Kingdom giving as a King - their **ministry must give as well,** not just personal giving. And the Lord said, **"I AM is raising up in these last days, a people who are Kings and Priests, not just one or the other. They will be about My Kingdom business in a BIG way. They will not think of themselves, but they will think of others and I WILL PROSPER THEM. They will not be about the bottom line, but they will only push forward and preach My gospel and Take the Land, by force, ALL for the Kingdom of God, says the Lord of Hosts."** We all have to be Spirit Led with our giving as well. So, be not adverse to the Lord telling you to give in new and unexpected ways.

Scripture References

--------⟨ • ⟩--------

*And hath made us **KINGS AND PRIESTS** unto God and his Father; to him be glory and dominion for ever and ever. Amen.* (Revelation 1:6 KJV)

*And hast made us unto our God **kings and priests:** and we shall reign on the earth.* (Revelation 5:10 KJV)

Give, and it shall be given unto you; good measure, pressed down, and shaken together, and running over, shall men give into your bosom. For with the same measure that ye mete withal it shall be measured to you again. (Luke 6:38 KJV)

*Religion that pleases God the Father must be pure and spotless. **You must help needy orphans and widows and not let this world make you evil.*** (James 1:27 CEV)

"THE PROVISION FOR YOUR VISION IS ON THE PATH THAT I HAVE SET BEFORE YOU, I AM TRANSLATING YOU FROM A SYSTEM OF COMPROMISE INTO KINGDOM SONSHIP"

2/23/2008

God is moving like never before in His Body. Many who think they have the truth will be shocked and very disappointed that they have put their hope in a building, a ministry, a Pastor, themselves or other things. These people and other things were not anointed to 'carry' our Hope. When we finally redirect our Hope to Jesus alone, we cannot and will not be disappointed. A paramount part of our walk with God is hearing His voice. We must hear His voice with 'Ears of True Understanding', so we CAN be Spirit led in ALL things, in ALL of life. Being Spirit led is what takes us from the burden of the law, into the **FREEDOM, and REST, of His Grace**.

The Bible tells us that the truth shall set us FREE. Sometimes, that 'truth', can be a painful thing for us to face. This is one of those Words that I really wrestled with God on... I was thinking that it may be a little harsh, so I waited. After a couple long days of waiting, the Lord told me to release it. He said, **"Now is the time for FREEDOM!"** You will not be able to read this Word without being changed! Lord, I pray that the Spirit of Truth and Understanding fall on your people. Allow them to receive the gift that You are giving them through this Word. In Jesus Name, Amen...

They will not frame their doings to turn unto their God: for the spirit of whoredoms is in the midst of them, and they have not known the LORD. (Hosea 5:4 KJV) In another version, the spirit name is different - *Their deeds won't allow them to turn to their God; for the spirit of prostitution is within them, and they don't know the LORD.* (Hosea 5:4 HNV)

I see a large tall wall, and at the top, and middle, of this wall is a door that is wide open. On the outside of this great wall I see endless stars and vast space with limitless and boundless opportunities - this represents the Generational Blessing of Abraham. Many of God's people are standing at the door that He has placed before them, and He has put a blindfold on them. Just behind them, there is a very small and restricted room of compromise and mediocrity where they have taken up residence and become quite comfortable, Luke warm even. This room can represent a job, a church, but also could be anything that we think we need, that will bring us sustenance, other than God alone. This room has kept many people right where they are at, stagnate and paralyzed, because it symbolizes some type of provision or self-fulfillment to them and they see this 'defiled provision' as their SOURCE instead of God. God considers this idolatry. For many, it has seemed like too much of a risk for them to **LET GO & TRUST HIM** - especially with their money. I can actually hear people saying, "Lord, you can have everything, but don't touch my money." Oh yes, we say God is our source, but do we really believe it in the depths of our hearts? You see, many of us do not even know what is in our own hearts and do not realize that fear is driving a 'survivalist mentality'. The Lord calls it a, **"Children of Israel Mentality."**

The Lord is about to reveal our own hearts to us. Many of us will be shocked and very disappointed at what is revealed. But, hear me when I say this - Do not worry, God is in control and He has us in His hands. He will not allow us to go through more than we can handle! *So let him who seems to himself to be safe go in fear* (take heed) *of a fall. You have been put to no test but such as is common to man: and God is true, who will not let any test come on you which you are not able to undergo; but he will make with the test a way out of it, so that you may be able to go through it. For this cause, my dear brothers, give no worship to false gods* (idols). (1 Corinthians 10:12-14 BBE)

What are we willing to have exposed to us about ourselves? And, what are we willing to give up for the call that Christ has placed on our lives? If our churches in buildings did not exist, what kind of **RELATIONSHIP** would we have with God? These will be questions that we will have to answer very soon. And the Lord said, **"For I am pruning My Body, cutting away, that which is not needed, that which is dead, that which will not bear good fruit, so My Body CAN produce the good fruit that honors Me."**

You see, we can be a people who 'plays church' and 'puts on an act', whenever and wherever we want. Some can see through this facade, but God always sees through it. No one fools Him, He sees our heart's motivation in all things. He is asking us to stop looking at each other, and the world, with **JUDGMENT** in our hearts, and to instead look at ourselves with **PERSPECTIVE.** The more honest we are with ourselves and the more willing we are to give up that which has a wrong place in our hearts, the easier this **'TRANSLATION'** will be. In fact, until we give something up in our hearts, we can never truly have it. Now is the time for us to Get Real and Grow Up In Christ. The Lord is asking us to give many things up (something that is or 'seems' truly important to us, or our 'Isaac') at a heart level this season. What is it that is our Isaac? And, can we let go of our Isaac? If we give it up at the heart level, we may not have to actually lose it. If the Lord is asking us to give up our Isaac, He is trying to set us up for the **Generational Blessing of Abraham.**

Each one of us has our own door that God is asking us to step through and trust Him completely because there is a very long drop if we were to fall from this height. And the Lord said, **"Just like a baby eagle is tossed out of its nest, so its instincts or intuition for flying can kick in, I am pushing My people through the door of FAITH, TRUTH and TRUST and into the next season - the season of DESTINY FULFILLED."**

And the Lord said, **"I have placed before you a door. Choose this day who you will serve, The Lord Your God, or mammon. I have gone before you and placed your provision, for your** vision, on the path that I have set before you. In this season I will 'Translate' you from A System of Compromise or Whoredom into Kingdom Sonship."

*For if you live according to the flesh, you shall die. But if you through the Spirit mortify the deeds of the body, you shall live. For as many as are led by the Spirit of God, they are the sons of God. For you have not received the spirit of bondage again to fear, but you have received the Spirit of adoption by which we cry, Abba, Father! The Spirit Himself bears witness with our spirit that we are the children of God. And if we are children, then we are heirs; heirs of God and joint-heirs with Christ; so that if we suffer with Him, we may also be glorified together. For I reckon that the sufferings of this present time are not worthy to be compared with the coming glory to be revealed in us. **For the earnest expectation of the creation waits for the manifestation of the sons of God.*** (Romans 8:13-19 MKJV) We are 'children of God' until we Grow up and become Spirit led, then we are 'Sons of God'. Read Philippians 2:12-16.

The Lord then said, **"My people, you have THREE chances to step through this door on your own, for this is NOT a door that you can ignore and 'miss the opportunity'. This door will CUT OFF the compromise, the compromise that has been a part of your lives for so long that you can't even see it as compromise anymore. This door is a door that you will have to go through, even if I have to push you through it Myself and close the door behind you, just know, it will be a smoother transition for you if you Trust Me and go through this door on your own. Any time someone gets paid to Compromise it is Whoredom. If you are not in the original and true predestined purpose that I have planned for your life, it is compromise - it is elusive and hidden, but I will reveal these hidden deceptions that the enemy and pride have so deviously intertwined into your life. I will show you what the correct timing is and when to make that move through this door and I will tell you where to go and what to do. Do not fear, I will catch you, I will catch you, I will catch you - for in this season I am also initiating the LAW of INTUITION. This will heighten your discernment to a level** that you have never witnessed before. Your instincts will be sharper, you will have a greater insight into the spirit realm and your 'ESP', Extra Spiritual Perception, will skyrocket as you take this next step of faith and come where I am, for where I am is the UNDEFILED PROVISION that you now seek. Truly, SEEK ME FIRST and PUT ME FIRST and the provision you seek for your vision will be there waiting for you on this next route of access, for I have set the course for the direction that I want your life to take. Watch and see what I will do - for many of you have a much greater destiny, than you have ever imagined or have seen, and you are about to WALK in TRUTH and LIVE in TRUTH and you are about to see it come to pass for my NAMES SAKE and my GLORY. Be ready and watch for this door - this door of FAITH, TRUTH and TRUST, for you will have to walk through it in the next two months, within the next two months - this is the manifestation of what you have prayed for and what you have labored over. The time is upon you now, your time is now - listen for My voice and be ready to make your move, Says the Lord of Hosts." The next two months is from the time you read this.

The Lord gave me the word **'Reordering'.** With this Apostolic reordering, He is putting things in our lives into the 'order' they should go in. He also revealed to me that in stepping through this door we are coming back into Covenant with Him, especially in the area of our finances. And, we are being delivered from idolatry in all areas of our lives - then He can bring 'The Great Wealth Transfer'. We have been going to the world's system for too long - for something the Lord wants to provide for us and give to us. God's system is one that GIVES and then those things will simply be added to us. The practical application in God's system is this: we give - this could be money, clothing, or a smile - whatever you have to give to meet the needs of others, and by the way, give to non-Christians also, there is no discrimination or wrong judgment in the Kingdom. (I am giving this Word to you right now - this is something God gave to me as a gift, I am passing it on to you). Not for glory for ourselves, but for the advancement of the Kingdom and for His glory - He makes sure we are taken care of. This doesn't mean we do not work, it means that our work is not first in our hearts **and** it is not about the money. If we are desperate for money we are in poverty, which is actually pride. Pride is when we see ourselves as our source instead of God. God resists the proud. When we truly put God first in our hearts, His FAVOR can be with us. With God's favor we will be simply amazed at how much easier life can be. We will still have the trials of life, but we are 'able' (the anointing goes before us) to overcome more easily than ever before.

The Lord wants us to know **'The Nature of a Shepherd'.** He is our Shepherd. The Shepherd goes down the path the night before the journey and sets 'provision' out for the sheep along the path, so it will be there as the sheep 'take the steps' (follow and obey what the Shepherd tells them). All they have to do, is follow the Shepherd and their provision will meet up with them as they come upon it. If the sheep continually disobey the Shepherd and decide not to trust Him, they would starve. Or, if they decide to go off on their own and become part of their own system, or the 'wolf's system' (organized religion), they will eventually get eaten. A good question to ask ourselves is, "where are our riches?" Are they in the Kingdom - putting others above self and giving unconditionally, all for the call of Christ? Giving unconditionally IS loving unconditionally, because you have to give to truly love. Or, are our riches in the money and the things of this world? *"If you love me, you will obey my commandments.* (John 14:15 GNB) BE SPIRIT LED UNDER THE NEW COVENANT.

Take a look at the Hireling contrasted with the Shepherd - the hireling will leave the sheep and run away, but the Shepherd will protect the sheep. Also, the sheep know the Shepherd's voice, but are 'confused' by the hireling's voice. Too often churches have had hirelings instead of Pastors. The enemy has been convincing people to have a survivalist mentality, so they stop giving, then the ministers have to be paid for their time right? It is a trap! No wonder so many are lost even if they are saved! They don't know they can hear God's voice for themselves and the Shepherds are nowhere to be found...

I am the door. If anyone enters in by Me, he shall be saved and shall go in and out and find pasture. The thief does not come except to steal and to kill and to destroy. I have come so that they might have life, and that they might have it more abundantly. I am the Good Shepherd. The Good Shepherd lays down His life for the sheep. But he who is a hireling and not the shepherd, who does not own the sheep, (This speaks of Dominion - if a leader understands Dominion they are a good Shepherd. Dominion was lost - the Lord is about to restore Dominion.) *sees the wolf coming and leaves the sheep and runs away. And the wolf catches them and scatters the sheep. The hireling flees, because he is a hireling and does not care for the sheep. I am the Good Shepherd, and I know those that are Mine, and I am known by those who are Mine. Even as the Father knows Me, I also know the Father. And I lay down My life for the sheep. And I have other sheep who are not of this fold. I must also lead those, and they shall hear My voice, and there shall be one flock, one Shepherd. Therefore My Father loves Me, because I lay down My life so that I might take it again. No one takes it from Me, but I lay it down from Myself. I have authority* (dominion) *to lay it down, and I have authority to take it again. I have received this commandment from My Father. Then a division occurred again among the Jews because of these words. And many of them said, He has a demon and is insane. Why do you hear him?* (John 10:9-20 MKJV)

It is interesting how the 'religious crowd' said that Jesus had a demon and then there was a 'church split'. God is refining His house! He has been speaking to me about His ministers not begging for or taking money **'To'** minister. It defiles the ministry and then they end up being 'hirelings'. They end up seeing money as their source and not God. It is okay to 'receive money in a church' or some other place - it is the 'wrong place money can have in our hearts' that can defile us. The Lord does not want us to 'Prostitute the gifts'. When we will 'not minister unless we get paid for it' or if we are 'desperate about money in our hearts in connection with ministry' it defiles the gifts and allows pride to get in. Pride comes with a lying and a blinding spirit. This is what makes a false prophet - the spirit of pride. If someone gives a love gift, that is a different thing, Paul was telling people to help support the ministers, but they shouldn't have to beg for money or ask for tithes. People should just give because it is the right thing to do - it is what the Kingdom is made of, selflessly giving and receiving in LOVE. The Lord has been talking about the hireling prostituting the gifts. When I looked up the definition of a hireling, this is what I found, hireling - mercenary; a prostitute. And, mercenary - One that may be hired; actuated by the hope of reward; moved by the **love of money.** (The love of money is the root of all evil) Greedy of gain; selfish.

Earlier in this chapter I mentioned **'Apostolic Reordering'.** This is what the Lord shared with me about this - the body of Christ is now coming into a season of total reliance and Trust in the Lord, a 'Blind Faith' (Blindly Walk by Faith) kind of Trust, where we cannot see the next steps in front of us, but we have only to rely on His voice and His hand to gently nudge, guide and lead us. Do Not get ahead of God. He is teaching us by His Spirit to respect **His ORDER of Authority** in the earth. This **respect for His Order of Authority is the ABILITY for functionality in the Body**. It is what allows the Flow of the anointing - then we can be in Alignment, so the flow can happen unhindered. The Order is this: *He that descended is the same also that ascended up far above all heavens, that he might fill all things. And he gave some, **Apostles**; and some, **Prophets**; and some, **Evangelists**; and some, **Pastors** and **Teachers**; For the perfecting of the saints, for the work of the ministry, for the edifying of the body of Christ:* (Ephesians 4:10-12 KJV)

When we observe His Order and His way of doing and being, Spirit led in all of life, on a heart level, we will see His GRACE, Kingdom Government, Unity, Love and Understanding invade the earth as never before. We will finally SEE the Kingdom. It has been there all along, we just couldn't SEE it until now. Christ IN us the Hope of Glory in the Earth. God Bless you all. Amen…

Scripture References

God blesses those people who depend only on him. They belong to the kingdom of heaven! (Matthew 5:3 CEV) He is trying to give us the Kingdom.

Truly, truly, I say to you, He who does not enter into the sheepfold by the door, but going up by another way, that one is a thief and a robber. But he who enters in by the door is the shepherd of the sheep. The doorkeeper opens to him, and the sheep hear his voice, and he calls his own sheep by name and leads them out. And when he puts forth his own sheep, he goes before them, and the sheep follow him. For they know his voice. And they will not follow a stranger, but will flee from him, for they do not know the voice of strangers. Jesus spoke this parable to them, but they did not understand what it was which He spoke to them. Then Jesus said to them again, Truly, truly, I say to you, I am the door of the sheep. All who came before Me are thieves and robbers, but the sheep did not hear them. I am the door. If anyone enters in by Me, he shall be saved and shall go in and out and find pasture. The thief does not come except to steal and to kill and to destroy. I have come so that they might have life, and that they might have it more abundantly. I am the Good Shepherd. The Good Shepherd lays down His life for the sheep. But he who is a hireling and not the shepherd, who does not own the sheep, sees the wolf coming and leaves the sheep and runs away. And the wolf catches them and scatters the sheep. The hireling flees, because he is a hireling and does not care for the sheep. **I am the Good Shepherd, and I know those that are Mine, and I am known by those who are Mine.** (John 10:1-14 MKJV)

And I will make your seed to multiply as the stars of the heavens, and will give to your seed all these lands. And in your Seed shall all the nations of the earth be blessed, (Genesis 26:4 MKJV)

For I know the purposes which I am purposing for you, says Jehovah; purposes of peace and not of evil, to give you a future and a hope. (Jeremiah 29:11 MKJV)

Beloved, I wish above all things that thou mayest prosper and be in health, even as thy soul prospereth. For I rejoiced greatly, when the brethren came and testified of the truth that is in thee, even as thou walkest in the truth. I have no greater joy than to hear that my children walk in truth. (3 John 1:2-4 KJV)

And to the angel of the church in Philadelphia write: He who is holy, He who is true, He who has the key of David, He who opens and no one shuts; and shuts and no one opens, says these things: I know your works. Behold, I have given before you an open door, and no one can shut it. For you have a little strength and have kept My Word and have not denied My name. (Revelation 3:7-8 MKJV)

*He who has an ear, let him hear what the Spirit says to the churches. And to the angel of the church of the **Laodicea** write: The Amen, the faithful and true Witness, the Head of the creation of God, says these things: I know your works, that you are neither cold nor hot. I would that you were **cold or hot.** So because you are lukewarm, and neither cold nor hot, I will vomit you out of My mouth. Because you say, I am rich and increased with goods and have need of nothing, and do not know that you are wretched and miserable and poor and blind and naked, I counsel you to buy from Me gold purified by fire, so that you may be rich; and white clothing, so that you may be clothed, and so that the shame of your nakedness does not appear. And anoint your eyes with eye salve, so that you may see. As many as I love, I rebuke and chasten; therefore be zealous and repent. Behold, I stand at the door and knock. If anyone hears My voice and opens the door, I will come in to him and will dine with him and he with Me. To him who overcomes I will grant to sit with Me in My throne, even as I also overcame and have sat down with My Father in His throne. He who has an ear, let him hear what the Spirit says to the churches.* (Revelation 3:13-22 MKJV)

Then Jesus said to the disciples, "And so I tell you not to worry about the food you need to stay alive or about the clothes you need for your body. Life is much more important than food, and the body much more important than clothes. Look at the crows: they don't plant seeds or gather a harvest; they don't have storage rooms or barns; God feeds them! You are worth so much more than birds! Can any of you live a bit longer by worrying about it? If you can't manage even such a small thing, why worry about the other things? Look how the wild flowers grow: they don't work or make clothes for themselves. But I tell you that not even King Solomon with all his wealth had clothes as beautiful as one of these flowers. It is God who clothes the wild grass---grass that is here today and gone tomorrow, burned up in the oven. Won't he be all the more sure to clothe you? What little faith you have! So don't be all upset, always concerned about what you will eat and drink. (For the pagans of this world are always concerned about all these things.) Your Father knows that you need these things. Instead, be concerned with his Kingdom, and he will provide you with these things. "Do not be afraid, little flock, for your Father is pleased to give you the Kingdom. Sell all your belongings and give the money to the poor. Provide for yourselves purses that don't wear out, and save your riches in heaven, where they will never decrease, because no thief can get to them, and no moth can destroy them. For your heart will always be where your riches are. (Luke 12:22-34 GNB)

Speak to the sons of Israel and command them that they make fringes in the borders of their garments throughout their generations, and that they put upon the fringe of the borders a ribbon of blue. And it shall be to you for a fringe, that you may look upon it and remember all the commands of Jehovah, and do them; and so that you do not seek after your own heart and your own eyes, after which you prostitute yourself, that you may remember and do all My commands, and be holy to your God. I am Jehovah your God, who brought you out of the land of Egypt, to be your God. I am Jehovah your God. (Numbers 15:38-41 MKJV)

My people *ask counsel at their stocks, and their staff declareth unto them: for the spirit of whoredoms hath caused them to err, and they have gone a whoring from under their God.* (Hosea 4:12 KJV)

For He has delivered us from the power of darkness and has translated us into the kingdom of His dear Son; in whom we have redemption through His blood, the remission of sins. (Colossians1:13-14 MKJV)

"I AM THAT I AM, I HEAR A SOUND OF FREEDOM & THAT OF A NEW HOPE, 2010 - A YEAR OF NEW LIFE & NEW PERSPECTIVE, IN CHRIST THE HOPE OF GLORY"

12/9/2008

I hear the Lord saying, over and over, **"There is a strategy for this season. The last shall be the first and the first shall be the last. The power to get wealth is in your midst for wealth is simply the absence of poverty. There is a new sound I hear says God, a sound of Freedom and that of a New Hope coming to My people - a hope that will not fail them like the hope that has failed them in the past. The hope that they have had has been a hope that has focused on the wrong things and on other people. Hear what I say, This is ALWAYS the formula for disappointment."** *The man whose heart is unmoved* (whose mind is stayed on You) *you will keep in* (perfect) *peace, because his HOPE IS IN YOU.* (Isaiah 26:3 BBE) The words in parentheses in the scripture above are taken from the (KJV).

And the Lord said, **"I AM is teaching you, My people, by My Spirit to respect authority - this respect for authority IS the ABILITY for functionality in the Body, and then you can be in alignment, so the flow can happen unhindered. Where there is no respect for authority, there is NO ANOINTING and NO PEACE. If your Mind and Focus stays on Me, respect for authority will just come without any effort - it will Just Be."**

Then He said, **"The reason why people do not just give respect, is because they have been focused on other people and what they are doing, or not doing, and not on Me alone. They have put their Hope in other people and not in Me. They have taken a False Responsibility for others actions and decisions and not trusted Me, concerning them. My people have been in a sleeping stupor, a trance of Jezebel and Rebellion and I will AWAKE them. Wake Up, Wake Up, Wake Up!!!"**

Then the Lord said, **"The Great Awakening has already begun, for it began in your month of November, 2009. The year of 2010 is a year of harvest. First it must come in the spirit realm, then it will manifest in the natural. I am bringing a fullness to not only the Gifts of the Spirit, but first the Fruits of the Spirit must be manifest in your hearts, and then the Harvest - then the Harvest. Be ready and prepare your hearts, for the harvest is coming says the Lord of Hosts."** Many of us think the Harvest is only 'good things', like finances or material items, but that kind of thinking is not truth. The harvest can also be a reaping of what we have sown. You would not sow an apple seed and expect corn to come up - what is it that we have sown? The Lord releases the Harvest according to what is happening in the Spirit Realm and what is happening in us at the Heart Level. Sometimes, it even means Justice and Judgment (the righteous kind of Justice and Judgment from the Lord - still, this can be a painful process). Either way, it means FREEDOM, because truth will prevail.

And the Lord said, **"I AM is changing your perspective, for everything that would ever be Given, has ALREADY been given. The answer you search for is already there and when I change your Perspective you will SEE it clearly, for the answer you seek is already in existence and is in fact right in front of you. Take it, Take it, Take it, Says the Lord of Hosts."** The Lord wants us to understand what the term 'I AM' actually means. I AM means - to be present in all things and live presently, I AM healed, I AM whole, I already HAVE this or that. He IS, that He IS. He wants us to JUST BE. *Therefore be careful how you hear. For whoever HAS, to him shall be given; and whoever HAS NOT, from him shall be taken even that which he seems to have.* (Luke 8:18 MKJV)

And the Lord said, **"You must HAVE something in your heart to actually possess it. Want implies lack, so DECIDE that you Have it and you will possess it. For MY ways are not your ways and My thoughts are not your thoughts. My realm is not subject to your realm, for your realm contains the five limited** dimensions of Length, Width, Height, Space, and Time. Where I am taking you there are NO dimensions - it is free and undeniably everywhere and every-time. Open your minds up, and you will see the manifestation of MY GLORY for the year of 2010 is a Year of New Life. It is a year of expectancy and anticipation, but instead of being disappointed again you will have your expectancy in Me and not in other people or things. A New Beginning has taken root in your hearts. I have been taking you through this process of cleansing, forgiveness and through 2009 'The Year of New Beginnings', so I could accomplish a new foundation in your hearts. I have done this so you could have a sturdy and strong foundation in which to build on for what I am about to bring to you. A new beginning making way for a new life, Life IN Christ, says God." Most of us will go through this process at different times - some did not see this until 2010 and others will not go through this until 2011.

And the Lord said, "I have released My Jeremiah prophets in the earth in 2009 to begin laying My groundwork. These are My prophets who are not worried about people pleasing and who have been tearing down what is not of Me. They are not very popular to the religious stronghold of Jezebel in people, especially religious Christians. In fact the Jezebel in people sees these prophets as being 'off'. This year of 2010 will be a year of re-building the Body, for the foundation that I am putting in you is that of a Clear Vision of the Cross, a perfect vision of Love, and that is the foundation that will cause you to UNDERSTAND being IN Christ. This Hope I speak of is being 'IN Christ, the hope of glory in the earth'."

And the Lord said, "There is a 'New Fire' anointing that I am bestowing on those who are FRIENDS OF GOD. This Three Part Anointing has already started to be released. It has the Joshua prophetic anointing - the Warriors in God's Prophetic Army, advancing and taking the land for the glory of the Lord. It has the Joseph prophetic anointing - those that have been in the pit, in bondage or imprisoned will now go FREE and go to the Palace." This is a change in status and also deals with the

Great Wealth Transfer. And He said, **"And it is also has the Jeremiah prophetic anointing - an anointing that roots out, pulls down, destroys, and throws down that which is not of God, and then plants and builds back up on the foundation of Pure and True Unconditional Love."**

There have been some key principalities and powers in certain parts of the land, especially the waterways, and God is ready to reveal them and flush them out! They have taken root in some major waterways (water is needed to support life). They have been trying to pollute, squeeze and snuff the life out of people!

And the Lord said, **"I will expose the false Apostolic and the True Apostolic will start to take their places of Authority in the earth - there will be A Changing of the Guard. A word to these, My Prophets, Jezebel will not like that you are speaking Truth into the hearts of My people. When you are opposed, simply Stand in Love and in Peace and do not be moved, the threats will dissipate. DO NOT FEAR, for FEAR IS AFRAID OF YOU, Trust Me and call its bluff!"**

And the Lord said, **"These Friends of God are those that would give up Everything for My purposes. These are people who have already been going through the process of giving things up and pulling down what is not of Me in their own hearts. For this Obedience of Sacrifice, I am going to bring these people to a New realm of Authority as this New Year of 2010 is birthed** (The Lord showed me that this will start manifesting in the natural realm in 2011)**. These anointings together make up a threefold cord that will not be broken, but will be able to break All Yokes of the enemy, Without Travail! Because these Friends have obeyed Me and put their heart up as a sacrifice, just as Abraham did with Isaac, I will not only give them this threefold anointing, but I will also release the Generational Blessing of Abraham to them. It doesn't matter where you come from, it doesn't matter what happened in your life, you will now have My favor and with My favor you will accomplish that which they said could not be accomplished for**

I hear a Sound of UNITY coming. UNITY is coming to young and old, to black and white, to all people of all races and all beliefs, and I the Lord will do it, you just simply Love and Live, Love and Live, Love and Live, says the Lord of Hosts." When the Lord says, **"Love and Live,"** it means, to truly Love is to Love Unconditionally, no matter who the person is and no matter what shape they seem to be in. To truly Live means, to Be Present, not living in the past or the future but in the NOW, truly living and enjoying our lives and not just surviving.

And the Lord said, **"I am releasing to you the Great Wealth Transfer with True Wealth, for True Wealth is Shalom. Money is just a byproduct of wealth. Stop focusing on the money."** This is a symptom of poverty, when someone goes after the things instead of keeping their focus on God it equates to idolatry. Then He said, **"If you continue to focus on the money and go after the money, you will NEVER get any, I have designed it that way."** The Lord gave me a vision of two magnets that are turned the wrong way and when you try to put them together they just push each other apart. It is this way with EVERYTHING THAT WE THINK WE NEED BESIDES HIM ALONE - it repels away from us and then we have a sense of rejection, lack and poverty. Then He said, **"Focus on Me says God, for I will cause the money, and people and things to be attracted to you, but you must have your heart right first."**

Then He added, **"If My people constantly Focus on the past, they will never ever be able to see the future."** God is delivering us from the root of poverty, so when He gives us this wealth we will not have a **'survivalist mentality'** with it and end up abusing it, and or making it an idol. Remember, money is a magnifier of whatever is in a person's heart. The Lord gave me a Word (see previous chapter) that spoke of translating us from **'Whoredom into Kingdom Sonship'** - this is what the prophet Jeremiah was talking about when people had brought other things into the **CENTER OF THEIR FOCUS** instead of God. *Long ago you broke off your yoke and tore off your bonds; you said, 'I* *will not serve you!' Indeed, on every high hill and under every spreading tree you lay down as a prostitute.* (Jeremiah 2:20 NIV®)

This is the Strategy for this Season that will Break the Yoke of Poverty...

1. Give to the poor and those in need - whatever the need may be. *He that giveth unto the poor shall not lack: but he that hideth his eyes shall have many a curse.* (Proverbs 28:27 KJV) *If you make money by charging high interest rates, you will lose it all to someone who cares for the poor.* (Proverbs 28:8 CEV)

2. Make sure your Focus is on God Alone, Confess any sin, especially idolatry, to mammon or other things that may have had a wrong place in your hearts, and allow Him to cleanse your heart. *Therefore take no thought, saying, What shall we eat? or, What shall we drink? or, Wherewithal shall we be clothed? (For after all these things do the Gentiles seek:) for your heavenly Father knows that ye have need of all these things. But seek ye first the kingdom of God, and his righteousness; and all these things shall be added unto you.* (Matthew 6:31-33 KJV) *No man is able to be a servant to two masters: for he will have hate for the one and love for the other, or he will keep to one and have no respect for the other. You may not be servants of God and of wealth.* (Matthew 6:24 BBE) *If we confess our sins, he is faithful and just to forgive us our sins, and to cleanse us from all unrighteousness.* (1 John 1:9 KJV)

3. Be willing to Give Up anything and everything for or to God as an Obedience of Sacrifice, especially your Isaac - this will make you a Friend of God. This shows the proof of your Faith or Belief in God at the heart level. It will also break off the spirit of Unbelief. Also, do Not be a friend to this world or the things of this world. *Does some stupid person want proof that faith without deeds is useless? Well, our ancestor Abraham pleased God by putting his son Isaac on the altar to sacrifice him. Now you see how Abraham's faith and deeds worked together. He proved that his faith was real by what he did. This is what the Scriptures mean by saying, "Abraham had faith in God, and God was pleased with him." That's* *how Abraham became God's friend. You can now see that we please God by what we do and not only by what we believe.* (James 2:20-24 CEV) *Yet even when you do pray, your prayers are not answered, because you pray just for selfish reasons. You people aren't faithful to God! Don't you know that if you love the world, you are God's enemies? And if you decide to be a friend of the world, you make yourself an enemy of God.* (James 4:3-4 CEV) *And Jesus answered and said, Truly I say to you, There is no man that has left house or brothers or sisters or father or mother or wife or children or lands for my sake and the gospel's sake, but he shall receive a hundredfold now in this time, houses and brothers and sisters and mothers and children and lands with persecutions, and in the world to come, eternal life. But many that are first shall be last; and the last shall be first.* (Mark 10:29-31 MKJV)

4. Work with God, and not against Him, when He tries to cut something off that has a wrong place in your heart. Submit to God. Being Mature in Humility and Having the Fruit of the Spirit operating in your life is God's Glory in the earth - this IS being IN Christ, IN CHRIST THE HOPE OF GLORY. *I am the true vine and my Father is the gardener. He takes away every branch in me which has no fruit, and every branch which has fruit he makes clean, so that it may have more fruit. You are clean, even now, through the teaching which I have given you. Be in me at all times as I am in you. As the branch is not able to give fruit of itself, if it is not still on the vine, so you are not able to do so if you are not in me. I am the vine, you are the branches: he who is in me at all times as I am in him, gives much fruit, because without me you are able to do nothing. If a man does not keep himself in me, he becomes dead and is cut off like a dry branch; such branches are taken up and put in the fire and burned. If you are in me at all times, and my words are in you, then anything for which you make a request will be done for you. Here is my Father's glory, in that you give much fruit and so are my true disciples.* (John 15:1-8 BBE) *But once a person has learned to have faith, there is no more need to have the Law as a teacher. All of you are God's children because of your faith in Christ Jesus. And when you were baptized, it was as though you had put on Christ in the same way you put on new clothes. Faith in Christ Jesus is what makes each of you equal with each other, whether you are a Jew or a Greek, a slave or a* *free person, a man or a woman. So if you belong to Christ, you are now part of Abraham's family, and you will be given what God has promised.* (Galatians 3:25-29 CEV) *(For the fruit of the Spirit is in all goodness and righteousness and truth), Proving what is acceptable to the Lord. And have no fellowship with the unfruitful works of darkness, but rather reprove them.* (This speaks of the 'works' of darkness, it is not talking about people - if we push people out of our lives, how then will we ever get close enough to reach them with the love of Christ? Separate the person from the sin, love the person and hate the sin.) *For it is a shame even to speak of those things which are done by them in secret. But all things that are reproved are made manifest by the light, for whatever makes manifest is light.* (We carry His light in us and our presence shines the light in darkness - we expose the spirit and love the people.) *Therefore he says, "Awake, sleeping ones! And arise from the dead, and Christ shall give you light." See then that you walk circumspectly, not as fools, but as wise, redeeming the time, because the days are evil. Therefore do not be unwise, but understand what the will of the Lord is* (by knowing His word and hearing His voice). (Ephesians 5:9-17 MKJV) *The secret which has been kept from all times and generations, but has now been made clear* (this is Him changing our perception) *to his saints, To whom God was pleased to give knowledge of the wealth of the glory of this secret among the Gentiles, which is Christ in you, the hope of glory:* (Colossians 1:26-27 BBE)

5. Show Love and Respect to ALL people and DO NOT JUDGE. Give Respect, especially to Authorities. The Lord said, "This is the Ability for Functionality in the Body." The flow will be unhindered and Unity will, and can, come. *Obey the rulers who have authority over you. Only God can give authority to anyone, and he puts these rulers in their places of power. People who oppose the authorities are opposing what God has done, and they will be punished.* (Romans 13:1-2 CEV) *I therefore, the prisoner of the Lord, beseech you that ye walk worthy of the vocation wherewith ye are called, With all lowliness and meekness, with longsuffering, forbearing one another in love; Endeavoring to keep the unity of the Spirit in the bond of peace. There is one body, and one Spirit, even as ye are called in one hope of your calling; One Lord, one faith, one baptism, One God and Father of all, who is above all, and through all, and in you all. But* *unto every one of us is given grace according to the measure of the gift of Christ. Wherefore he saith, When he ascended up on high, he led captivity captive, and gave gifts unto men. (Now that he ascended, what is it but that he also descended first into the lower parts of the earth? He that descended is the same also that ascended up far above all heavens, that he might fill all things.) And he gave some, apostles; and some, prophets; and some, evangelists; and some, pastors and teachers; For the perfecting of the saints, for the work of the ministry, for the edifying of the body of Christ:* (This speaks of Order of Authority and observing this Order is what brings Peace and Unity) *Till we all come in the unity of the faith, and of the knowledge of the Son of God, unto a perfect man, unto the measure of the stature of the fullness of Christ:* (In Christ, producing fruit) (Ephesians 4:1-13 KJV)

The Father Is Calling...
Religion Or Relationship???
6/22/2010

Many of us have been walking through seemingly very terrible times. They have been very painful, very scary times where we can't seem to see the road two feet ahead of us. For many this is terrifying, because we are used to being in complete control at all times and have never Really been asked to **TRUST GOD COMPLETELY**. Most of us do not understand the very fine line that exists between **what is our responsibility and what is God's responsibility in our lives and in the lives of others**. This is one reason why some of us see Him as a **'wish monger'**, His words, not mine, instead of a Father. Many of us grew up in this **'Fatherless Generation'** where the Father figure was either absent, or, if he was around, he was an alcoholic, abusive, not present, or lacked the understanding of how to teach **Respect, Order, Discipline, Discretion, Timing and Dominion.** All of these are very important tools that are part of having a well-rounded and balanced Godly life.

'Religion' has taught us to take the path of **least resistance** and if things are going wrong, well then, we must be on the wrong path, right? We may think that taking the path of least resistance would be the way to go, but God is looking for a lot more **TRUST** out of us than that. **Without TRUST and RESPECT there is no Relationship.** Without relationship there is nothing. The road that Relationship is on is a trying one, but it is more than worth it, because this is where **True FREEDOM Lives**. When you **'go through'** with someone (in this case God), it creates a **TRUST** that wouldn't be there otherwise.

In this season, God is looking to change our **Head Knowledge of who "I AM" is, into a Heart Understanding** and Translate us from a System of Compromise into Kingdom Sonship. He also wants to teach us the real role of a Father, since many have never had the opportunity to have a real father figure before. Then we will be able to **see Him as our Father and as our Source for all that we need or desire.** It is then, that we will really start to **LIVE LIFE** instead of just survive it. To Trust In Him with all of our hearts will take some refining, and **refining is a painful process.** It involves taking a hard, long look at our own hearts, not to condemn ourselves or to feel guilty, no - it is to **be honest with ourselves and with God.** When we do this and Trust Him with our hearts, **healing and restoration will soon follow.**

I almost made a horrible mistake this past weekend and looked to the world's system, and man's limited understanding, for a very delicate situation in my own life. You see, **EVERYTHING has a spiritual root** and if we are only treating the symptoms of a thing, with man's system that is set up to 'make money' off of people who are in need, we will always be stuck in bondage and in the same place - in slavery and stagnant. **We have been denying His power because we haven't truly believed Him...**

Many of us will 'want' to stay right where we are because it is comfortable to us - we have become accustomed to the rut we have been in. The problem with this is, when we become accustomed to something in this way, it can then become our SOURCE instead of God. If we translate this out, it is equal to **idolatry.** I know this sounds harsh, but it is true.

God is looking to pull us out of our rut and give us **New Life In Him, No more accepting generational ailments and curses, complete FREEDOM!!!** I remember hearing someone say, "Christians are the sickest and most messed up people they knew." I know God's people are longing and groaning in their hearts for this Freedom and I know it can be a scary thing to think about, but we need not worry or be afraid. God has us in His hands and He will not forget us, leave us, or forsake us. The enemy is only fighting us this hard because he can see that we are about to **POSSESS THE LAND!!!!**

Once we start this Journey with the Lord, He tells us, **"NEVER LOOK BACK!"** As we start to 'come out' (of the rut) and begin the refinement process, remember, it will be painful and even **seem like loss to us** and the temptation is to 'look back' to our former place of comfort, but **do not do it!** I hear the Lord saying, **"DON'T LOOK BACK, DON'T LOOK BACK, DON'T LOOK BACK!"** Remember what happened to Lot's wife when they were coming out of Sodom and Gomorrah? She looked back and turned to a pillar of salt! When I was seeking the Lord about this He showed me that this 'system' He is talking about is in direct correlation with Sodom and Gomorrah. If you remember, Sodom and Gomorrah was a city where homosexuality prevailed and fornication was thought of as something you just do. The Lord revealed to me that homosexuality and fornication, in essence, is the spirit of **REBELLION.** God's original design was to make man and then to make a woman to be with man - not man to be with man. And, He made **One** man to be with only **One** woman in the sanctity of marriage. He showed me that these **roots are REBELLION and LUST.** God is looking to **rid us of any and all Rebellion and any Lust on a HEART LEVEL. This LUST is the LUST OF Mammon** (includes homosexuality and fornication - a way for us to provide ourselves stimulation in sin) **or Money.** Mammon is not our Source or our God! Jehovah is our Source or Provider and our God! Again, **Money is just a tool**.

God is beginning the **process of FREEDOM** in our lives. Do not look back to a system that has enslaved us and made us its bond servants. Do not be turned to a pillar of salt that has lost its savor, good for nothing, but to be thrown out and to be trodden underfoot by men. We need to listen carefully to the Father and follow His Voice and stay close to Him, like a sheep would stay close to the Shepherd (sheep like sustenance and protection), so we don't get **eaten by the wolves**.

I see judgment coming to the world's system for being the 'replacement' for the Father in our lives - it is made up of people with man's pride, ideals, and pursuit of mammon and the powers and principalities that exalt themselves against God. I see the Lord raining 'fire' down on it, and it will start with the established 'man's church system' and then we will see it in the world's system starting with the drug companies. If we continue to be a part of the world's system, we may get burned just from the 'fall out'. **You may see a lot of persecution when you go down the RIGHT PATH, still, GO towards FREEDOM - RUN TO THE FATHER! HE IS WAITING FOR US WITH OPEN ARMS!** There is **Pain in the Process**, but God is our protector and our comforter. Do not go to people with something you should go to God with, you will likely be **MISLED.** Do not fear, HE IS FOR us and if He is for us, who can be against us? No one, and, No thing!!!

I am by no means getting down on Fathers. There are many Fathers out there that have done a wonderful job raising their children and sometimes other people's children also. Part of this 'alignment process', that we are going through right now, is to finally understand how to put our **HOPE IN HIM ALONE and find our Identity In Christ.**

Scripture References

And when the dawn rose up, then the angels hurried Lot, saying, Rise up! Take your wife and your two daughters who are here, lest you be consumed in the iniquity of the city. And he lingered, the angel laid hold upon his hand, and upon the hand of his wife, and upon the hand of his two daughters (Jehovah being merciful to him), and they brought him forth and set him outside the city. And it happened when they brought him outside, He said, Escape for your life! Do not look behind you, nor stay in all the plain. Escape to the mountain lest you be consumed. And Lot said to them, Oh no, Lord, please now, Your servant has found grace in Your sight, and You have magnified Your mercy, which You have shown to me in saving my life. And I cannot escape to the mountain, lest some evil take me and I die. Behold now, this city is near to flee to, and it is a little one. Oh let me escape there (is it not a little one?) and my soul shall live. And He said to him, See, I have accepted you concerning this thing also, that I will not overthrow this city for which you have spoken. Hurry and escape there! For I cannot do anything till you have come there. Therefore the name of the city was called Zoar. The sun had risen upon the earth, and Lot entered into Zoar. Then Jehovah rained upon Sodom and upon Gomorrah brimstone and fire, from Jehovah out of the heavens. And He overthrew those cities, and all the plain, and all the inhabitants of the cities, and that which grew upon the ground. But his wife looked back from behind him, and she became a pillar of salt. (Genesis 19:15-26 MKJV)

Blessed are they who have been persecuted for righteousness sake! For theirs is the kingdom of Heaven. Blessed are you when men shall revile you and persecute you, and shall say all kinds of evil against you falsely, for My sake. Rejoice and be exceedingly glad, for your reward in Heaven is great. For so they persecuted the prophets who were before you. You are the salt of the earth, but if the salt loses its savor, with what shall it be salted? It is no longer good for anything, but to be thrown out and to be trodden underfoot by men. (Matthew 5:10-13 MKJV)

Behold, I have set the land before you: go in and possess the land which the LORD sware unto your fathers, Abraham, Isaac, and Jacob, to give unto them and to their seed after them. (Deuteronomy 1:8 KJV)

HOPE, NEW BEGINNINGS & WONDERMENT, "I HAD TO CLOSE THE OLD BOOK OF YOUR LIFE TO BRING YOU TO NEW LIFE IN ME"

4/8/2010

And the Lord said, **"This is a new season, one that has started out in a hurtful place - a place of birthing for you, and it has been a very painful and lonely place. I am here and I understand the pain you have suffered and the tears you have cried, for I have kept your tears, and I will turn them into blessing very soon. This season will now turn to a season of Hope, New Beginnings and Wonderment - a time to get to know Life with a New outlook, as if you were an infant learning life all over again. I had to close the chapter on the Old Book of Your Life in order to bring you the New Life that I have in store for you. The innocence that was once lost, will be restored. You will see things from a New perspective. You will not lose any of the Wisdom that life's lessons have brought you, but, as you are already aware, I have been healing your heart to it's very core. Be still and listen carefully, for I am teaching you My ways, from My frequency. My voice is still, subtle and quiet - you will have to be very still to hear it, as still as a fawn in the brush when a predator is near. I am training you to hear My voice where I speak and where the enemy cannot pick it up - In My frequency** (at the vibration where God resides). **Be aware My child, for the imps plagued your line for generations, do Not allow them in for they put on a big display, but they are very small in the light of what you already are In Me. Fasting and Praying will be a strategy for you in this season. Be an observer of the happenings around you. Speak only when I release you, move only when I release you. I am teaching you the precise timing in all things, for when I release you, you will be as the very Word itself, a two-edged sword, piercing even to the dividing apart of soul and spirit, and of the joints and marrow, and a discerner of the thoughts and intents of the heart. Be still and know, Be still and know, says the Lord of Hosts."** The Lord gave me the scripture, Hebrews 4:12 to go along with this Word.

Scripture References

God is in the midst of her; she shall not be moved; God shall help her at the turning of the morning. The nations raged, the Kingdoms were shaken; He uttered His voice, the earth melted. Jehovah of Hosts is with us; the God of Jacob is our refuge. Selah. Come, behold the works of Jehovah, who makes ruins on the earth; who makes wars to cease to the ends of the earth, He breaks the bow, and cuts the spear in two; He burns the chariots in the fire. Be Still and know that I am God! I will be praised among the nations, I will be praised in the earth. Jehovah of Hosts is with us; the God of Jacob is our refuge. Selah. (Psalms 46:5-11 MKJV)

GOD'S TRUE GLORY IN THE EARTH EQUATES TO US GIVING TO, FOR, & ON OTHERS BEHALF, PAIN IS THE PROCESS OF POWER

7/10/2010

This is what **'bearing one another's burdens'** means - we stand in the gap and **GIVE,** we give whatever is needed. Love first, then Faith, or Hope - we stand in the gap and be the **'stand in'** in ALL Humility, because at the time they are not able to do it for themselves. There are many out there that cannot GIVE because they are either too perplexed or they are too prideful. It takes Humility to truly Give. As we stand in the gap and **GIVE on their behalf FIRST**, it will start the process of **GRACE** in their lives. We do this for them until they learn that they themselves can Give, even while they are still in an infirmity. Remember when Paul asked God to take the thorn out of his side? God said, **"My Grace is sufficient for you, for My Power is made perfect in weakness."** Then Paul said, **"Then I would rather Glory IN my infirmities - SO THAT the Power of Christ may rest upon me."** Paul was 'weak' or humbled. So, we humble ourselves and **Glory/Give** in an infirmity **especially when it hurts** and then His **Grace/Power** shows up. We can be the one to Glory or Give, on others behalf, in the time of their need when their faith would wavier because of fear. His Glory IS Us Giving TO, FOR, and ON others behalf... **We ARE FREE to Give!**

For if I desire to boast, I shall not be foolish. For I will speak the truth. But I spare, lest anyone should think of me as being beyond what he sees me, or hears of me; and by the surpassing revelations, lest I be made haughty, a thorn in the flesh was given to me, a messenger of Satan to buffet me, lest I be made haughty (prideful)*. For this thing I besought the Lord three times, that it might depart from me. And He said to me, My grace is sufficient for you, for My power is made perfect in weakness* (humility)*. Most gladly therefore I will rather glory in my weaknesses, that the power of Christ may overshadow me. Therefore I am pleased in weaknesses, in insults, in necessities, in persecutions, in distresses for Christ's sake; for **when I am weak,*** (humbled) *then I am powerful* (Because it is God's power on us, not our own). (2 Corinthians 12:6-10 MKJV)

You see, we do not have to be bound to thinking that we are suffering, **even if we ARE**. God is trying to get His power to us, the anointing - **the ability to be made into His image and Step into our Calling**. We can gain an Understanding that **we have the Power to choose our reactions and our actions,** to what may or may not be happening, at a heart level - this is being Mature and Christ-like. His **Grace** allows us to be able to choose our reactions and actions in any circumstance. We have all been 'trained' to complain when things are going 'wrong'. I would say, everything is actually 'right' all the time. This is because God is working things out for our Good and His Glory. The **'going through'** infirmities and things that perplex us is the technique God uses to Humble us and to **gain access** our hearts. Hard times should humble us. **If hard times make us angry or make us 'freak out' there is Pride present.** The quicker we humble ourselves the quicker the 'trial' will be over.

And he that searcheth the hearts knoweth what is the mind of the Spirit, because he maketh intercession for the saints according to the will of God. And we know that all things work together for good to them that love God, to them who are the called according to his purpose. For whom he did foreknow, he also did predestinate to be conformed to the image of his Son, that he might be the firstborn among many brethren. Moreover whom he did predestinate, them he also called: and whom he called, them he also justified: and whom he justified, them he also glorified. What shall we then say to these things? If God be for us, who can be against us? (Romans 8:27-31 KJV)

MONEY IS THE LITMUS TEST! SON'S OF GOD OR SLAVES TO MONEY? HARVEST WILL BE REVEALED AS HE BECOMES FIRST, KINGDOM SONSHIP AWAITS!

8/23/2010

The Bible says that the Lord chastens (redirects our path of) those that He loves. This message is a very hard, painful truth that ALL of us will have to face at some point very soon. I pray the Lord reveals Himself to us all in a new way, enlightening the eyes of our hearts, so we will allow Him to begin the cleansing process in us at a heart level. It is when we submit to this process, that He will finally become the **High Priest** in our lives, taking our Head Knowledge of Him and Translating it into a Heart Knowledge of who **I AM** truly is. It is in this transformation that we will find our **TRUE identity IN CHRIST** and finally Understand what it means to **HAVE the MIND of CHRIST**. You see, the **Mind of Christ** does not exist in our carnal minds but is only known in the depths of our hearts, for He has written His Words on our hearts. He is looking for us to surrender our hearts to Him and allow Him to cleanse us of ALL unrighteousness. This is all He really wants from us in the first place, our hearts, in their entirety.

There are a couple questions that keep emanating from God, for us to ask ourselves in this season, "Are we Sons of God?" Or, "Are we slaves to Money (mammon) and eventually Sin?" If we are not Spirit Led in ALL of life in ALL that we do or don't do, then we are not Sons of God yet. We can be 'children' of God without being 'Sons' (I don't care how many church services we go to, or how much we 'serve' at church, **Going to church is not a substitute for a Spirit led life**). Are we following the money train? Are we caught up in a dead end job that has nothing to do with our true destiny, the destiny that God created for us? If the source (what we 'think' is our source - like a job) of our money were removed from us like it has been for so many, would we 'freak out'? If any of the answers to the three questions above are, "yes," then we should ask ourselves, "are we Sons, and IN

Christ?" Or, "is there still some area of lack or poverty in our hearts?"

The poverty mindset gives no Glory to God on any level and is based on the fear of not 'having', but being in 'want' or 'lack'. *A Psalm of David. Jehovah is my Shepherd; I shall not want.* (Psalms 23:1 MKJV) If the Lord is truly our Shepherd (leading us and guiding us in all things - hence the Spirit led life), then we will not want for anything because it is **already provided by the Shepherd**.

Are we 'getting paid' (in this case, 'getting paid' is the **main reason or heart motivation to do** His work) **to use** the precious gifts that God has gifted us with for HIS GLORY? If so, then we are 'Prostituting the Gifts'. Ouch! I Know! Or rather, if we will not use our gifts unless we get paid to do so, we are in lack or poverty. Poverty is what causes people to prostitute themselves out for money in any aspect of life (compromising truth values or dignity for money because we don't trust God to provide for us). This mindset has been defiling God's people to the very depths of their hearts since Adam sinned in the Garden (I am talking about Spiritual Gifts and some talents, but mostly the gifts of the Spirit). Poverty is simply this - not seeing God as our source for ALL things, and thinking **we** have to do it and get it, ALL for ourselves. Simply put, we do NOT Trust God to provide, protect, or to be our source for ALL things.

All of us should already be using our gifts in all of life, not just at 'church'. When we Step into HIS flow, **FREELY GIVING AWAY that which He has given to us,** using our gifts (IN ALL HUMILITY, because Pride perverts the gifts), then we will see that the Provision for our Vision was there waiting for us all along. The provision will be revealed to us as we take the steps of FAITH In Obedience, just like it was revealed to Abraham when he laid Isaac on the altar and was about to sacrifice him. God had already provided the 'provision' for Abraham in the form of a ram caught in the thicket. It is better to obey than to sacrifice, but when God gives us an opportunity to BOTH Obey and Sacrifice, He is setting us up for the **'Generational Blessing of Abraham'**.

Who, or What, is our Isaac? For most of us, it is where we get our money. It could be a job or a church or even a job at church. Are we willing to sacrifice our 'Isaac' on the altar of our hearts for God and His purposes and His true will for our lives? I am not talking about giving another 'church offering', I am talking about our sources of income - laying them down and saying, "Lord, is this Your Predestined Purpose for my life, or is there something more, slated out from the beginning of time, that was purposed for me to do and be?" It would be good in this season for us to ask the Lord who, or what, is our Isaac? He is asking us to give whomever, or whatever, up to Him **at a heart level, and see Him as our Source for Everything,** because **where our treasure is there will our heart be also...**

In this season, the Lord is Translating our Head Knowledge of who He is into a Heart Knowledge. For most of us, this will be a very painful process. It is a season of Job - the double portion, and a season of the Generational Blessing of Abraham. God does not want to allow Great Wealth in our lives until our hearts are right - money is only a TOOL, not our Focus, our FOCUS has to be on Him alone. **God designed everything in the Universe, so if something was our source besides Him, we would not be able to 'have it' - it is, in effect, cursed.** It is possible for us to possess something without actually having it, but there will always be lack and it will come with a sorrow or burden attached to it because we are trying to 'bless ourselves'. When we 'have' something that God has allowed, because our hearts are right, then it comes with blessing. Many have blessed themselves ahead of God and didn't allow Him to bestow the blessing on them. This **'blessing ourselves'** comes with a **sorrow or burden** on our shoulders and is a **symptom of the poverty mindset.** It is a form of pride and idolatry, because we are putting ourselves in God's place and giving to ourselves, when

we were created to Give to God and to others - then God and others give back to us.

God is infusing this KINGDOM way of being into the earth right now. Does this mean you can never buy anything for yourself again? No, I am speaking in a general sense. Recently, someone I know was so amazed when a woman gave him a postage stamp. Is this what we have come to? Someone else I know had to pay her sister back for a long distance phone call that cost only 50¢. Have we all gotten to the point where it is a 'big deal' to give anything, even something as small as a postage stamp or a 50¢ phone call, away to others? What if God asked us to give a car or a house away to someone? Could we do it? Could we do it with a cheerful heart? If there is **anything at all** that we 'can't give' when God asks us to give, then **we are still IN Poverty and IN Pride.**

Money is a magnifier or 'litmus test' to what is already in a person's heart. If God allowed us to have great wealth in the monetary, things or people sense, before our hearts where right, it would destroy us. He loves us too much for that to happen. We would also end up worshiping Mammon, or other people, and eventually we would lose all of it anyways. That is a by-product of poverty also 'loosing' what little we do have. *For whoever has, to him shall be given, and he shall have more abundance. But whoever does not have, from him shall be taken away even that which he has.* (Matthew 13:12 MKJV)

Christ alone has to be our Source, our Foundation and our FOCUS, then we will SEE that the Harvest was THERE ALL ALONG, it just hadn't been revealed to us until we were **ready to see it.** In all things and in all ways it comes back down to our hearts. HE wants our whole heart. Can we let go of things that have wrong places in our hearts, especially the love of money (the root of all evil)?

Mammon (money) and Entertainment have exalted themselves above God in 'our temples' and 'our churches'. Can we turn to the Lord and repent of idolatry and **REDIRECT our FOCUS** back to HIM? The time is NOW for God to Reign in our hearts. The Harvest will be revealed to us as soon as we **PAY NO HEED TO IT** anymore. When we can say, "The money and the things and the people are **NOT** my source, and LORD, No Matter what I have to go through, You alone are my source and my sustenance, in You alone will I TRUST!!!" Then the Harvest! Then the Harvest! Our redemption draws nigh as we heed to His Will and His Way and **ASK HIM WHAT WE ARE SUPPOSED TO BE DOING WITH THE LIFE HE HAS GIVEN US.**

If we were NOT Sent specifically by HIM to GO, DO, JOIN or ATTEND, then we are IN Pride (effected by a religious spirit), Out of His Will or Out of Order. This is what defines a false prophet. So many of God's people have followed the latest 'protest' or 'cause' or joined the 'trendiest church', without seeking the Lord first. Let's Seek Him in **ALL** things. He can be Trusted, if we seek Him we will find Him - He promises that. And, He will guide us through this transition from a **SYSTEM OF COMPROMISE** (Whoredom) **into KINGDOM SONSHIP...**

And the Lord said, **"Your redemption draws nigh, for behold I will do a NEW THING - I will cause the well to spring up from the depths of your spirit. I will make a way in the wilderness and in the winter of your year 2010 / 2011, I will cause things to turn around to your favor. As you turn from Mammon and turn your Focus to Me, says God, I will carry you, I will save you, I will honor you. I will do it for My Namesake and My Glory. TRUST and OBEY, TRUST and OBEY and SEEK ME FIRST, AND YOU SHALL FIND ME, says the Lord of Hosts."**

Scripture References

And you have forgotten the exhortation which speaks to you as to sons, "My son, despise not the chastening of the Lord, nor faint when you are rebuked by Him; for whom the Lord loves He chastens, and He scourges every son whom He receives." If you endure chastening, God deals with you as with sons, for what son is he whom the father does not chasten? But if you are without chastisement, of which all are partakers, then you are bastards and not sons. Furthermore we have had fathers of our flesh who corrected us, and we gave them reverence. Shall we not much rather be in subjection to the Father of spirits and live? For truly they chastened us for a few days according to their own pleasure, but He for our profit, that we might be partakers of His holiness. Now chastening for the present does not seem to be joyous, but grievous. Nevertheless afterward it yields the peaceable fruit of righteousness to those who are exercised by it. (Hebrews 12:5-11 MKJV)

For as many as are led by the Spirit of God, they are the Sons of God. (Romans 8:14 MKJV)

I say, then, Walk in the Spirit and you shall not fulfill the lusts of the flesh. For the flesh lusts against the Spirit, and the Spirit against the flesh. And these are contrary to one another; lest whatever you may will, these things you do. But if you are led by the Spirit, you are not under law. (Galatians 5:16-18 MKJV)

The blessing of Jehovah itself makes rich, and He adds no sorrow with it. (Proverbs 10:22 MKJV)

Ask and it shall be given to you; seek and you shall find; knock and it shall be opened to you. (Matthew 7:7 MKJV)

AFRICA - A NATION AMONG NATIONS, I WILL START WITH YOU & SET YOU 'A-FIRE' WITH MY 'NEW FIRE'

10/21/2010

The Lord said, **"AFRICA, A Call to Repentance, A Nation among Nations - for you have suffered and I have seen your suffering, now rise oh Mighty Nation, take your place, for I will set you 'A-Fire' with My 'New Fire'. Turn to Me and away from your sins and I the Lord your God will heal your Land and heal your Bodies, for the sins that have cursed the land for generations will be forgiven and your land will yield its crop and you will be a fruitful land and they will say, 'Jehovah has done this'. I will start with you oh Africa and My power and My glory will overtake the entire Earth. Look for it, look and be glad - Run to Me and I will do it for My Namesake and My Glory says the Lord of Hosts."**

"I Am Sending My Mighty Rushing Winds Of Change! Get Ready, For Revival Is In Your Midst!!!"

10/26/2010

I had a vision today and it was of God - He was taking a deep breath and blowing a mighty wind across the Mid-West (of the United States). He turned towards me and said, **"I am sending My Mighty, Rushing Winds of change, for you have suffered and you have asked, 'Where is our Hope'? Hear what I say, enough of this! Your hope is being restored even now and I will start with the HEART-LAND of this Great Nation, America, America - My 'New Israel' and you will SEE My TRUE Salvation and you will SEE the Harvest for My Namesake and My Glory, says the Lord of Hosts."**

*And in the fulfilling of the day of Pentecost, they were all with **ONE ACCORD IN ONE PLACE**. And suddenly a sound came out of the heaven as borne along by the rushing of a mighty wind, and it filled all the house where they were sitting. And tongues as of fire appeared to them, being distributed; and it sat upon each of them.* (Acts 2:1-3 MKJV)

And the Lord said, **"Get ready, for REVIVAL is in our Midst!!!"**

I saw this wind blowing the demonic influences away and I kept seeing giant baskets of apples falling from the sky. These apples symbolized harvest, but these baskets were huge and overflowing and there were so many. The Lord showed me that pride comes with a blinding spirit and that the harvest has been there all along, but **we couldn't SEE it because of the pride.** All of these trials were meant to humble us and teach us how to humble ourselves. As we walk in **HUMILITY** the blinders are taken off, especially off the eyes of our hearts and we can SEE what has **ALREADY BEEN GIVEN** - through the **Work of the**

Cross and the GRACE of God. We ARE FREE - the Harvest IS HERE!!!

Thank you Lord, now to **practice humility, and LOVE and Keep our FOCUS on Jesus!** That is where it is at - **The Secret Place, our place of Provision and Protection!!!**

HANG ON! HANG ON! BEHOLD, THE HAPPENING OF THE GREAT AWAKENING IS HERE, A SEASON OF ABUNDANCE IS NOW UPON YOU

11/9/2007

Hang On, Hang On, Hang On, Breakthrough is on the way! I keep seeing things being one way one day, struggling, downcast and almost a feeling of being disheartened, and the very next day I see things turned around - **OVER NIGHT!** We will have the capability to carry God's POWER for His Glory - blessing beyond belief, prosperity, double portion, anointing and wealth transfer, health being restored, families restored and everything that was lost will be restored, and then some!

This past season was a season of stretching, pulling and making us malleable so we can withstand the light and the heat of His GLORY that we will now be able to carry. This was also for the ability to carry great wealth - we had to be **stretched in the financial realm of our Minds Thinking** and our **Hearts Motivation**. This all for the harvest that was here all along - we just could not SEE it yet. **The Happening of the GREAT AWAKENING is now spreading around the World.**

The Lord said, **"The Understanding that had escaped you since the Resurrection will now be known at a Heart level. No more doubt! No more fear! I will be in you and all around you and you will Exude and Permeate My Glory in all the Earth. You have been going through what you have felt is hell on earth. I had to allow this to teach you Humility. Humility is the KEY that will Protect you as you Traverse the Terrain that is coming ahead of you. Hold On! Relief is coming! I say again, Hold On! Relief is coming! You will see this relief in the coming few months, before the end of your year 2010. This will be the greatest Christmas of blessing that you have ever seen, especially Spiritually. Expect to see your loved ones trickling into the Kingdom in your year of 2011. Those who were not blessed in October were not forgotten - no, not by any means.**

These are my Jobs - I am refining them to a greater purpose and a greater Glory. These are my Sons in who I am well pleased - these are the Josephs who will stand for Truth and Justice and will not compromise my Word for the sake of people's approval. These are a people who I have purposely chosen to Promote in this next season and they will, oh yes, they will be receiving the DOUBLE PORTION in this next season - a season of blessing and abundance, for My Namesake and My Glory, says the Lord of Hosts."

The double portion is going to be in whatever areas you have had the most struggles in - in this past season.

Also remember that there is no time or space limitation in the Spirit realm. Just because there is a 'date' listed above doesn't mean that this was the only time that He can bless you. This is for you when you read it and receive it.

Because you got a double dose of trouble and more than your share of contempt, Your inheritance in the land will be doubled and your joy go on forever. (Isaiah 61:7 **THE MESSAGE**)

WATCHMEN ARISE & WARN OF JUDGMENT TO COME, PRIDE THE 'MARK' OF A FALSE PROPHET

10/10/2010

Once in a while the Lord has something to say and it is chastening in nature... This is one of those times. As you read this Word keep in mind that I am taking this to heart in all humility and searching my own heart first. I would never release a Word that I haven't first taken an honest look at my own heart and judged myself.

Lord, I pray that You will give all who read this Word a heart understanding of what You are conveying here. Give us Grace to turn to the path that we were predestined to be on IN Christ Jesus. Thank you Lord for your unconditional love, in Jesus Name, Amen.

It is important to remember that God loves us. If you pick up on any 'holy anger' in this Word, it is directed towards the spirits involved and not the people. He is showing us where we have been off the path and telling us where to 'course correct' so we can get back on the path that He has predestined for us, the path that holds His BEST for our lives. We, as people, have a will. He is asking us to **turn again** to Him. This is a season of **dying to self** and our Pride has GOT TO GO! The Lord wants to give us His GRACE. **As we die to self and find our HUMILITY, we will find His REST and in HIS REST is where we will find His GRACE and POWER as a result.**

*When Your people Israel are crushed before the enemy because they have sinned against You, and shall **turn again** (this implies an act of our will) to You and confess Your name, and pray, and cry to You in this house, then hear in Heaven and forgive the sin of Your people Israel, and bring them again into the land which You gave to their fathers. When the heavens are restrained, and there is **no rain** because they have sinned against You, if they pray toward this place and* *confess Your name, and turn from their sin **when You afflict them,** then hear in Heaven and forgive the sin of Your servants, and of Your people Israel, for **You shall teach them the good way in which they should walk,** and give **rain on Your land** which You have given to Your people for an inheritance.* (1 Kings 8:33-36 MKJV)

The scripture above is NOT speaking of a head knowledge of Him or a 'works based' system, it is talking about our **hearts**. What is in our hearts? Are they turned towards HIM? Are we HIS on a heart level, or is it just an outwardly or intellectual appearance? He wants our **Whole Heart and ALL of our Trust**. If we are truly His, then we will obey His Voice - His Sheep follow Him and they **know** His Voice. Are we Spirit led in ALL things and in ALL of our ways? *My sheep hear My voice, and I know them, and **they follow Me.*** (John 10:27 MKJV) This scripture implies hearing God's VOICE - not just from the written Word, but hearing His voice with the **Ears of True Understanding** and then **OBEYING** what He says to **do, say, be, and live**. This is when His GRACE kicks in. This is our part in Covenant with Him.

Recently, the Lord told me that He would be revealing to me who the **'false prophets'** really are. Then I began to see very subtle, yet bad fruit. I never thought I would see it in the places that I did. It was so subtle in fact, that I almost missed it. If it were not for the Lord revealing some things to me, I would never have seen it.

And the Lord said, **"I am calling on those who I have previously called out and hidden away, My sheep that I have hidden away in their caves - caves filled with the Refiners Fire, those who have tasted the fruit of hopelessness only to Turn Again to Me and find their HOPE IN Me alone. Those who have had their hearts broken and then turned their Focus towards Me - My Watchmen... I AM is calling on them for they are needed for such a time as this. They are needed to call out the corruption and to bring a Word of Warning to the**

'established church.' This is not to condemn, but to bring chastening (redirect our path - because He loves us) **and to put them on the true path, My path.** Pride in the form of Mammon and Entertainment have exalted themselves in My temple, not only in the church building, but in people's hearts everywhere. Man has stolen My GLORY - it has taken on the appearance of false humility, but hear what I say, this is still pride. The wolves have taken over and are deceiving and being deceived. The true wolves do not know they are wolves, but you will know them by their fruit. Their fruit is the fruit of pride. Where you do not see the fruit of true love you will see this foul selfish and self-righteous fruit. The true wolves are afraid to be deceived by the wolves. They are marked by this pride and by the 'pursuit of mammon'. You see, if you know the Truth the Truth WILL set you FREE! If you are not FREE then you haven't been fed the truth. If you KNOW the TRUTH, you CAN NOT be deceived. My Sheep know My voice. I say again, My Sheep KNOW My voice. Many who walk the halls of the 'established church' are very 'busy' doing what they think they should do for Me, yet they have not sought Me first to see if it was something that I want them to do. Many who walk these halls are very busy trying to 'save the lost', yet they themselves need saving. I ask you, how can you help those that you sit in judgment against - YOU CAN NOT - this is the opposite of Unity. This is the gospel of hatred and rejection and I will put up with it no more! You shall SEE My True Kingdom come and you shall see it come with demonstration of My 'New Fire', My Grace and My Power such as the world has never seen before! No more, 'Man Spirit', no more 'One Man Show', no more 'Business As Usual', no more 'Status Quo', no more 'Good Ol' Boys', no more 'Mediocrity' - The days of the 'Powerless House of God' ARE OVER, says the Lord of Hosts."
Revival is coming!!! It is coming as we Turn Again - as we turn back to the One True God Jehovah, put Him first in our hearts and minds, listen to His voice, get our Marching orders from Him alone, and execute the orders He gives us.

Then the Lord asked, **"What is it that makes a false prophet?"** He said, **"It is simply the spirit of PRIDE. Pride can make a**

115

normally true prophet, Temporarily False." The Lord has been revealing a lot to me about pride. Pride is basically, an impoverished mindset, **seeing ourselves as our source for our needs and desires** (this translates to idolatry) instead of **waiting on the Lord to provide** for us and **seeing Him as our source for everything in ALL of life.**

When we DO NOT SEE God as our source, we then, **'feel rejection'** - the response is fight or flight. We usually run from God because fighting with Him is pointless until we realize that there is really **nowhere to run from Him...** When we finally get the revelation of the fact that God is truly our source for everything, our experience will become, **'AS IF ADAM HAD NEVER SINNED'.** The work of the Cross has done this for us. As we begin to understand this, we will believe it and then receive it. **This is True Salvation.** *We will know the truth and the truth will make us FREE.* (John 8:32 paraphrased)

If we are not **totally FREE** then we haven't gotten a hold of the **UNDERSTANDING of the TRUTH.** There may be some who are reading this and might be getting offended by it, that is actually a good test to see if pride is present. **Where offense is present, there is also pride present.** Just remember, none of us can run from God. We will have to change or we will fall and we will fail, over and over again until we surrender to His will and his way. *Pride goes before destruction, and a haughty spirit before a fall.* (Proverbs 16:18 MKJV) The Lord wants us all to Turn Again to HIM, Humble ourselves before His mighty hand and **TRUST HIM** to be our source for everything in all of life.

Pride perverts the gifts and allows a lying and a blinding spirit to get in. I am finding that it is all coming down to, **"Are we truly restored to the Father?"** Or, **"Are we truly saved?"** If we are, then we see Him as our source for everything - not other people or things. He uses people to bless us by His hand, but they are not our source. We should not be running to man in fear and begging for bread. *I have been young, and am old; yet I have not* *seen the righteous forsaken, or his seed begging bread.* (Psalms 37:25 MKJV)

If a prophet (or ANYONE bringing the Word of the Lord) is in pride in any way, comparing themselves to others, inferring that they are better in some way, competing with others, gossiping, asking for money to minister or all too willing to take money from people (but then when those same people are in need they turn their back on them), backbiting, jealousy, people pleasing, needing acceptance, bragging, ministries laying out snares for the sheep (in attempt to 'see' their fruit because they cannot discern in the Spirit to actually 'test the spirits' the true Biblical way) - these are manifestations of the fruit of pride. When people are grumbling and whining about 'going through', this is a fruit of pride as well.

This scripture puts it quite well. *Know this also, that in the last days grievous times will be at hand. For men will be self-lovers, money-lovers, boasters,* **proud***, blasphemers, disobedient to parents, unthankful, unholy, without natural affection, unyielding, false accusers, without self-control, savage, despisers of good, traitors, reckless,* **puffed up***, lovers of pleasure rather than lovers of God,* **having a form of godliness, but denying the power of it;** *even turn away from these. For of these are those who creep into houses and lead captive silly women loaded with sins, led away with different kinds of lusts,* **ever learning and never able to come to the full knowledge of the truth** (these are Not people who have not touched a Bible - the scripture just said ever learning, that means they have been studying the truth but haven't come to the full knowledge of it). *But as Jannes and Jambres withstood Moses,* (rebellion against authority) *so these also resist the truth, men of corrupt mind, reprobate concerning the faith.* **But they shall proceed no further. For their foolishness shall be plain to all***, as theirs also became. But you have fully known my doctrine, manner of life, purpose, faith, long-suffering, love, patience, persecutions, afflictions, such as happened to me at Antioch, at Iconium, at Lystra.* **What persecutions I endured! But the Lord delivered me out of all. Yea, and all who desire to live godly in Christ Jesus will be** *persecuted. But evil men and seducers will go forward to worse, deceiving and being deceived.* (2 Timothy 3:1-13 MKJV)

Remember God looks at the heart, this is not only an outwardly thing, what really counts is inwardly - what is in our hearts. Many 'look the part of sheep', but inwardly they are as ravenous wolves. *Go in through the narrow gate, for wide is the gate and broad is the way that leads to destruction, and many there are who go in through it. Because narrow is the gate and constricted is the way which leads to life,* (feeling 'constricted' lately?) *and there are few who find it. Beware of false prophets who come to you in sheep's clothing, but inwardly they are ravening wolves. You shall know them by their fruits. Do men gather grapes from thorns, or figs from thistles? Even so every good tree brings forth good fruit; but a corrupt tree brings forth evil fruit* (the **love of money** is the root of all evil). *A good tree cannot bring forth evil fruits, nor can a corrupt tree bring forth good fruit. Every tree that does not bring forth good fruit is cut down and thrown into the fire* (The refiner's fire). *Therefore by their fruits you shall know them.* (Matthew 7:13-20 MKJV)

The Lord is about to reveal the hearts of those that share the Word of the Lord. **Judgment is coming** to those who have handled His Word wrongly without the respect it deserves. Many have been blinded to the real Truth of the Word because of this pride and they have been teaching a **skewed version of truth** - which is in fact a lie. *A little leaven leavens all the lump.* (Galatians 5:9 MKJV) This causes people to have a *form of Godliness but deny the power thereof* (2 Timothy 3:5 paraphrased). **His true GRACE and POWER has been denied.**

There are two different 'churches' of God. There is the **'established man's church system'**, built around the **love of money** and there is the **true church** - those who have received Grace, truly repented and put God first in their hearts and minds. There are many who are a part of the true church who are attending 'man's church system' (God has a purpose for them being there). How do we know them? Well, their fruit will tell. One way to identify this 'man spirit' is when we see God's word compromised, desperation and panhandling for money (they think they are their own provider or source, not God). Another way to tell is **Law** versus **GRACE**. The Gospel of Grace is Power Unto Salvation - True Salvation, the power of the Cross. **If we are still trying to perform the law then we are still under the curse of the law.** *Then since we have such hope, we use great plainness of speech. And we are not like Moses, who put a veil over his face so that the sons of Israel could not steadfastly look to the end of the thing being done away. (But their thoughts were blinded; **for until the present the same veil remains on the reading of the old covenant, not taken away.) But this veil has been done away in Christ. But until this day, when Moses is read, the veil is on their heart. But whenever it turns to the Lord, the veil shall be taken away.** And the Lord is that Spirit; and **where the Spirit of the Lord is, there is liberty.** But we all, with our face having been unveiled, having beheld the glory of the Lord as in a mirror, are being changed into the same image from glory to glory, even as by the Lord Spirit.* (2 Corinthians 3:12-18 MKJV)

When we receive His Grace, then we **ARE FREE** from the curse of the law and our reality will become **'AS IF ADAM HAD NEVER SINNED'.** When Adam sinned and saw himself as his source (that is what sin is - focusing on someone or something else that is not God, it is Pride) he was thrown out of the garden and God was no longer his source (Because God resists the Proud). This caused Adam to have to be his own source and in turn he developed a **'poverty mindset'.** Jesus came to restore God as our Source and Eradicate this poverty mindset (it is a spirit). Most of us just haven't understood this until now. The Lord is dealing with this poverty in people's hearts and minds.

And the Lord said, **"I will UNITE these TWO churches and you will SEE MY POWER and My glory such as the World has never seen."** Here is the scripture on the **'two churches'.** *I am the Good Shepherd, and I know those that are Mine, and I am known by those who are Mine. Even as the Father knows Me, I also know the Father. And I lay down My life for the sheep. And **I have other sheep*** *who are not of this fold. I must also lead those, and they shall hear My voice, and there shall be ONE flock, ONE Shepherd. Therefore My Father loves Me, because I lay down My life so that I might take it again. No one takes it from Me, but I lay it down from Myself.* I have authority to lay it down, and I have authority to take it again. I have received this commandment from My Father. (John 10:14-18 MKJV)

He is asking us to lay down our lives so that we may take them again. This is the chance He is giving us to repent and turn away from this pride and the poverty mindset. *Incline your ear, and come unto me: hear, and your soul shall live; and **I will make an everlasting covenant with you, even the sure mercies of David.*** (Isaiah 55:3 KJV) He keeps saying, **"The Key to the House of David is yours, turn again to Me."**

*Come unto me, all ye that labour and are heavy laden, and I will give you **REST**. Take my yoke upon you, and learn of me; for I am meek and lowly in heart: and ye shall find **REST** unto your souls. For my yoke is easy, and my burden is light.* (Matthew 11:28-30 KJV) If we are heavily burdened, then we haven't found His **REST,** yet. This means we are **getting and doing it for ourselves and even trying to minister in our own power.** His burden is light - it is HIS burden **NOT ours.** If we are truly HIS, then HE is the one who is responsible for our needs to be met, we simply **TRUST and OBEY** and the provision will meet up with us on the path that HE has set before us, not the one we have set before ourselves. The only 'doing' that we should be 'doing' is to OBEY, His VOICE.

If we do not Trust Him, then we are in pride. It is only one way or the other, there is no 'middle of the road' here, a little bit of pride present is still pride, so Trust Him. So many of us do not realize that there are areas where we do not trust in Him until a trial comes, then we find out just how much we still do not trust. Trusting in the Lord is a confidence and a knowing, that no matter what the circumstance we face in life, the Lord is FOR US, and He will Provide for us and He is our source for ALL things. *For I know the plans I have for you, declares the LORD, plans to prosper you and not to harm you, plans to give you hope and a future.* (Jeremiah 29:11 NIV®) And the Lord said, **"If I would lay down My very LIFE for you, you should know you can TRUST ME to take care of your needs."** *But whom He predestinated, these He also called; and whom He called, those He also justified. And whom He justified, these He also glorified. What then shall we say to these things? If God is for us, who can be against us? Truly He who did not spare His own Son, but delivered Him up for us all, how shall He not with Him also freely give us all things? Who shall lay anything to the charge of God's elect? It is God who justifies.* (Romans 8:30-33 MKJV)

He is asking us to turn from our own devices and the way we have learned to 'survive' and believe HIM and truly begin to LIVE... *"I, the LORD, **refuse to accept anyone who is proud.** Only those who **LIVE BY FAITH** are acceptable to me."* (Habakkuk 2:4 CEV) *So then those of faith are blessed with faithful Abraham.* ***For as many as are out of works of the Law, these are under a curse;*** *for it is written, "Cursed is everyone who does not continue in all things which are written in the Book of the Law, to do them."* **(If you do just one part of the law you are then responsible for all of it.)** *But that **no one is justified by the Law** in the sight of God is clear, for, "The just shall live by faith." But **the Law is not of faith**; but, "The man who does these things shall live in them." Christ redeemed us from the curse of the Law, being made a curse for us (for it is written, "Cursed is everyone having been hanged on a tree"); so that the blessing of Abraham might be to the nations in Jesus Christ, and that we might **receive the promise of the Spirit through faith.*** (Galatians 3:9-14 MKJV)

*But He gives more grace. Therefore He says, **God RESISTS THE PROUD**, but He gives **GRACE TO THE HUMBLE.** Therefore submit yourselves to God. **RESIST THE DEVIL, AND HE WILL FLEE FROM YOU.*** (He has no power - whatever we FOCUS ON has power - so FOCUS ON JESUS.) ***Draw near to God, and He will draw near to you.*** *Cleanse your hands, sinners; and purify your* *hearts, double-minded ones. Be afflicted, and mourn and weep. Let your laughter be turned to mourning and your joy to heaviness. Be humbled before the Lord, and He will lift you up.* (James 4:6-10 MKJV) If we understand that God resists the proud then we know when someone is communing with God or not, based on the fruit of pride. When you see the fruit of Pride, do not listen to what is being said **at the time pride is present,** Only listen when you see the fruit of Humility. When we are proud He resists us - when we are in Humility He gives Grace, Power, Anointing and Ability... *Likewise, younger ones, be subject to older ones, and all being subject to one another.* **Put on humility.** *For God resists proud ones, but He gives grace* (power) *to the humble.* (1 Peter 5:5 MKJV)

The Lord wants us to know the difference between a hireling and a Shepherd. He said we have had hirelings in the pulpit instead of True Shepherds. The PLACE the money has had in the hearts of those ministering is what makes the difference. Is the money their source or do they TRUST God to provide for the ministry needs? *The thief does not come except to steal and to kill and to destroy. I have come so that they might have life, and that they might have it more abundantly. I am the Good Shepherd. The Good Shepherd **lays down His life for the sheep.** But he who is a **hireling and not the shepherd,** who does not own the sheep* (not responsible for the sheep), *sees the wolf coming and **leaves the sheep and runs away.** And the wolf catches them and scatters the sheep. **The hireling flees, because he is a hireling and does not care for the sheep.** I am the Good Shepherd, and **I know those that are Mine, and I am known by those who are Mine.*** (John 10:10-14 MKJV)

The Lord has been saying a lot about those who take money, for the use of their gifting that He has gifted them with, and saying that they are **'prostituting the gifts'** and how the **'hirelings'** have taken over in the **'man's church'** and made themselves fat. *And the word of the LORD came unto me, saying, Son of man, prophesy against the shepherds of Israel, prophesy, and say unto them, Thus saith the Lord GOD unto the shepherds; **Woe be to the shepherds of Israel that do feed themselves! should not the shepherds feed the flocks?** Ye eat the fat, and ye clothe you with the*

*wool, ye kill them that are fed: but **ye feed not the flock. The
diseased have ye not strengthened, neither have ye healed that
which was sick, neither have ye bound up that which was
broken, neither have ye brought again that which was driven
away, neither have ye sought that which was lost; but with
force and with cruelty have ye ruled them.** And they were
scattered, because there is **no shepherd:** and they became meat to all
the beasts of the field, when they were scattered. My sheep wandered
through all the mountains, and upon every high hill: yea, my flock was
scattered upon all the face of the earth, and none did search or seek after
them. Therefore, ye shepherds, hear the word of the LORD; As I live,
saith the Lord GOD, surely because my flock became a prey, and my
flock became meat to every beast of the field, because **there was no
shepherd, neither did my shepherds search for my flock, but the
shepherds fed themselves, and fed not my flock;** Therefore, O ye
shepherds, hear the word of the LORD; Thus saith the Lord GOD;
Behold, I am against the shepherds; and I will require my flock at their
hand, and cause them to cease from feeding the flock; neither shall the
shepherds feed themselves any more; for **I will deliver my flock from
their mouth,** that they may not be meat for them.* (Ezekiel 34:1-10
KJV)

I was shocked when I looked up the word hireling. This is the
definition of the word 'hireling' from Webster's dictionary - One
who is hired, or who serves for wages. A mercenary; a
prostitute. This is part of the definition of a mercenary -
Actuated by the **hope of reward; moved by the love of money.**
The Lord told me there are those who are 'prostituting' the gifts.
Wow! **It is not that we cannot receive something that is given
to us, it is about what is in our heart regarding the money. We
cannot be desperate for the money. Money is a tool, it is not
our source - GOD wants to be our SOURCE for everything.**
*THE YOUNG LIONS DO LACK, AND SUFFER HUNGER: BUT
THEY THAT SEEK THE LORD **SHALL NOT WANT** (Lack) ANY
GOOD THING.* (PSALM 34:10 KJV)

He said that the 'False Shepherds' or hirelings have led His
sheep astray. The Lord revealed to me that in **some** churches and

some 'deliverance ministries', they are focusing on the devil and demons and giving them way too much credit. They think they are helping people, but they are only causing more fear and more bondage. **The enemy is defeated - only if we focus on him does he have any power - WE ARE FREE!** Too often, ministries try to point out the 'wolves' and yet, they themselves are wolves. Remember, the wolves are afraid to be deceived by the 'wolves'. God showed me that the parallel is like the drug companies. God told me that if the drug companies truly did what they 'claim to do', they would go out of business. God showed me that their goal is not to truly 'help' people, but to keep them bound to 'maintaining' a certain level of bondage. Ouch! The same thing is happening in SOME churches and deliverance ministries! They fear truly getting you Set Free because they might 'lose your business' and their money. Ouch! Sorry to say this, but it happens - I've seen it. It is time for the Watchmen to arise and begin to warn people of what is coming. We need to check our own hearts and see where money has had its wrong place and turn away from the love of money and from pride. **JUDGMENT IS COMING! Judgment is simply a separation of the pure from the impure.** It can be a painful process, but if we do what the Lord is saying, it will be much easier for us.

There is an ORDER in the Spirit realm that has been lost in the 'church building'. Are all churches like this? I do not know, but here is the 'Order' of God's authority - in Order... *And truly He gave some to be **Apostles**, and some to be **Prophets**, and some to be **Evangelists**, and some to be **Pastors** and **Teachers**, for the perfecting of the saints, for the work of the ministry, FOR THE EDIFYING OF THE BODY OF CHRIST.* (Ephesians 4:11-12 MKJV) Does this mean that one is better than the other? No, but when we honor God's Order the anointing can flow unhindered. There have been Pastors who are trying to 'Lord' their authority over Apostles and Prophets and they have been **IN PRIDE AND OUT OF ORDER**. When we choose to ignore Order, the anointing (ability) is hindered because of Pride.

This is a call to the Watchmen Prophets to go forth and say what He says!!! Only what He says, and when! Also, like Jeremiah, do not look at their faces! We are not in it to 'people please', only to God please, and we have to stay in TRUST in HIM - This is the Secret Place - our place of Protection and Provision. If you have to question whether or not you are a watchman then you are not called at this point and at this time. *Rejoice and be exceedingly glad, for your reward in Heaven is great. For so they persecuted the prophets who were before you. You are the salt of the earth,* **but if the salt loses its savor,** *with what shall it be salted? It is* **no longer good for anything,** *but to be thrown out and to be trodden underfoot by men. You are the light of the world. A city that is set on a hill cannot be hidden. Nor do men light a lamp and put it under the grain-measure, but on a lamp stand. And it gives light to all who are in the house. Let your light so shine before men that they may see your good works and glorify your Father who is in Heaven.* (Matthew 5:12-16 MKJV) What is it that is our 'good works'? **To turn again to HIM with all of our hearts and minds...**

So to recap, give away that which He has given to you and He will take care of your needs. Be spirit led in ALL things and in ALL of your ways and you will meet up with the provision for your vision on the path that HE has led you down - this is where the 'undefiled' provision is. You can receive a 'love gift' of money as long as your heart is in the right place and you are not desperate for the money and the money is not a condition of ministering - it is merely a tool not our source. GIVE, GIVE, GIVE, GIVE! He will take care of you. Look out for others and He looks out for you. This is Kingdom!

Scripture References

———— ⌒ • ⌒ ————

Do not think that I have come to destroy the Law or the Prophets. I have not come to destroy but to **fulfill** *(Satisfy once and for all). For truly I say to you, Till the heaven and the earth pass away, not one jot or one tittle shall in any way pass from the Law until all is* **fulfilled** **(He has already fulfilled it by the Work of the Cross).** *Therefore* *whoever shall relax one of these commandments, the least, and shall teach men so, he shall be called the least in the kingdom of Heaven. But whoever shall do and teach them, the same shall be called great in the kingdom of Heaven.* (Matthew 5:17-19 MKJV)

My people have been lost sheep; **their shepherds have caused them to go astray;** *they have turned them away on the mountains. They have gone from mountain to hill; they have* **forgotten their resting place.** *All who have found them have devoured them. And their enemies said, We do not offend, because they have sinned against Jehovah, the habitation of righteousness, even Jehovah, the hope of their fathers. Flee from the midst of Babylon, and go out of the land of the Chaldeans, and be as the he-goats before the flocks. For, lo, I am stirring up and bringing up against Babylon a company of great nations from a northern land. And they shall array themselves against her. She shall be captured there. Their arrows shall be as those of a skillful, mighty man; none shall return in vain.* (Jeremiah 50:6-9 MKJV)

And Jehovah appeared to Solomon by night, and said to him, I have heard your prayer, and have chosen this place to Myself for a house of sacrifice. If I shut up the heavens, and there is no rain, or if I command the locusts to devour the land, or if I send a plague among My people; **If My people, who are called by My name, shall humble themselves and pray, and seek My face, and turn from their wicked ways,** *then I will* **hear from Heaven and will forgive their sin and will heal their land.** *Now My eyes shall be open, and My ears shall be open to the prayer of this place. For now I have chosen and sanctified this house, so that My name may be there forever. And My eyes and My heart shall be there forever. And you, if you will walk before me, as David your father walked, and do according to all that I have commanded you, and shall observe My statutes and My judgments, then I will make the throne of your kingdom sure, as I have covenanted with David your father, saying, There shall not fail you a man to be ruler in Israel.* (2 Chronicles 7:12-18 MKJV)

"Focus On Me - I Am Resurrecting The Old Seeds, The Power To Get Wealth Is In Your Midst"

3/20/2008

The Lord told me to merge this Word with another one, so you may have read parts of this before. He said the time for it is now. May God Bless you as you read it.

And the Lord said, **"Just as Christ Jesus was raised from the dead I am resurrecting the Old Seeds. I am bringing the harvest forth from these former dead seeds and I am declaring this a 'season of resurrection.' Unusual miracles will begin to take place especially in the financial arena. My POWER TRANSFER - not only for miracles of Healing and New Thinking, but also I will give you the Power to Get Wealth for TRUE WEALTH is simply the absence of Poverty. My people must die to themselves and their own ambitions so I can resurrect them to Live and Walk IN ME - In the TRUTH. For IN CHRIST IS WHERE THE BLESSING IS COMMANDED.** The 'Baal of Mammon' or 'God of Money' has been in many people's hearts and this must die out of their hearts. When money rules in a person's heart, they are In the 'Baal of Mammon'** (the god of Money) **and they are NOT IN Me. Raise your heads, FOCUS ON ME and allow Me to cleanse your hearts from ANY idol that may be there. Then My Power will come, then My Power will come! Do not straddle the fence on this one, with ME it is ALL or NOTHING. I want your Whole Heart! If I allow My People to attain the wealth without cleansing their hearts first, it would corrupt their lives and be destructive to them. Money is like a magnifier to what is already in a person's heart. If there is anything that is not of Me it would be magnified when the money is applied. If your heart is cleansed from idols then when the money is applied it will glorify Me. I AM will cleanse My people's entire hearts and by MY grace I AM cleansing MY temple from the 'money changers'** (Worldly goods and Greed). **I AM will make My People Holy and I AM will bring My people into a life of** prayer and make MY house a House of Prayer and a House of Power says the Lord of Hosts."

The Lord showed me a vision of His people who have already been positioning themselves for this Great Wealth Transfer and I saw them receiving **the 100 fold return** off of these Old Seeds, but then He said, **"Double Portion Also."** He said that this would be **100 fold X 2.** So, let's Focus on Him, and be open and willing to allow God to cleanse our hearts and follow Him where He leads us to go.

Scripture References

and so that you might not say in your heart, My power and the might of my hand has gotten me this wealth. But you shall remember Jehovah your God, for it is He who gives you power to get wealth, so that He may confirm His covenant which He has sworn to your fathers, as it is today. And it shall be if you do at all forget Jehovah your God and walk after other gods and serve them and worship them, I testify against you today that you shall surely perish. (Deuteronomy 8:17-19 MKJV)

Every man also to whom God hath given riches and wealth, and hath given him power to eat thereof, and to take his portion, and to rejoice in his labor; this is the gift of God. (Ecclesiastes 5:19 KJV)

But you will be named the priests of Jehovah; it will be said of you, Ministers of our God; you will eat the riches of the nations, and you will revel in their glory. For your shame you will have double; and for disgrace they will rejoice in their portion; therefore in their own land they will possess double; everlasting joy will be theirs. For I Jehovah love judgment, I hate robbery for burnt offering; and I will direct their work in truth, and I will make an everlasting covenant with them. (Isaiah 61:6-8 MKJV)

The Below verses on this page pertain to what can happen to a man who is not mature enough for the wealth, or has idols in his heart - it would destroy him. In this case it is vanity. The King James Version talks about vanity...

God may give you everything you want--money, property, and wealth. Then God doesn't let you enjoy it, and someone you don't even know gets it all. That's senseless and terribly unfair! You may live a long time and have a hundred children. But a child born dead is better off than you, unless you enjoy life and have a decent burial. That child will never live to see the sun or to have a name, and it will go straight to the world of darkness. But it will still find more rest than you, (Ecclesiastes 6:2-4 CEV)

There are people, for instance, on whom God showers everything-- money, property, reputation--all they ever wanted or dreamed of. And then God doesn't let them enjoy it. Some stranger comes along and has all the fun. It's more of what I'm calling smoke. A bad business. Say a couple have scores of children and live a long, long life but never enjoy themselves--even though they end up with a big funeral! I'd say that a stillborn baby gets the better deal. It gets its start in a mist and ends up in the dark--unnamed. (Ecclesiastes 6:2-4 ***THE MESSAGE***)

The Lord is throwing out the money changers and making His house - His temple a house of Prayer and Power... *And Jesus went into the temple of God, and cast out all them that sold and bought in the temple, and overthrew the tables of the moneychangers, and the seats of them that sold doves, And said unto them, It is written, My house shall be called the house of prayer; but ye have made it a den of thieves. And the blind and the lame came to him in the temple; and he healed them.* (Matthew 21:12-14 KJV)

Behold, as the eyes of servants look unto the hand of their masters, and as the eyes of a maiden unto the hand of her mistress; so our eyes wait upon the LORD our God, until that he have mercy upon us. (Psalms 123:2 KJV)

Choose you this day who you will serve...

I call Heaven and earth to record today against you. I have set before you life and death, blessing and cursing. Therefore, **choose life***, so that both you and your seed may live,* (Deuteronomy 30:19 MKJV)

Right now I call the sky and the earth to be witnesses that I am offering you this choice. Will you choose for the LORD to make you prosperous and give you a long life? Or will he put you under a curse and kill you? **Choose life!** (Deuteronomy 30:19 CEV)

For where your treasure is, there will your heart be also. The light of the body is the eye. Therefore if your eye is sound, your whole body shall be full of light. But if your eye is evil, your whole body shall be full of darkness. If therefore the light that is in you is darkness, how great is that darkness! **No one can serve two masters.** *For either he will hate the one and love the other, or else he will hold to the one and despise the other.* **You cannot serve God and mammon.** (Matthew 6:21-24 MKJV)

A good man out of the good treasure of the heart bringeth forth good things: and an evil man out of the evil treasure bringeth forth evil things. (Matthew 12:35 KJV)

that Jehovah may continue His Word which He spoke concerning me, saying, If your sons take heed to their way, to walk before Me in truth with all their heart and with all their soul saying, there shall not be a man of yours cut off from the throne of Israel. (1 Kings 2:4 MKJV)

Beloved, in regard to all things **I pray that you prosper and be in health, even as your soul prospers.** *For I rejoiced greatly when the brothers came and testified of the truth that is in you, even as you walk in the truth. I have no greater joy than these things, to hear that my children walk in the truth.* (3 John 1:2-4 MKJV)

The steps of a good man are ordered by the LORD: and he delighteth in his way (This is because he is Spirit led). *Though he fall, he shall not be utterly cast down: for the LORD upholdeth him with his hand. I have been young, and now am old; yet have I not seen the righteous forsaken, nor his seed begging bread. He is ever merciful, and lendeth; and his seed is blessed. Depart from evil, and do good; and dwell for evermore. For the LORD loveth judgment, and forsaketh not his saints; they are preserved for ever: but the seed of the wicked shall be cut off. The righteous shall inherit the land, and dwell therein for ever. The mouth of the righteous speaks wisdom, and his tongue talketh of judgment. The law of his God is in his heart; none of his steps shall slide. The wicked watcheth the righteous, and seeketh to slay him. The LORD will not leave him in his hand, nor condemn him when he is judged.* **Wait on the LORD, and keep his way, and he shall exalt thee to inherit the land: when the wicked are cut off, thou shall see it. I have seen the wicked in great power, and spreading himself like a Green Bay tree** (the Green Bay Tree a symbol of wealth and wickedness). **Yet he passed away, and, lo, he was not: yea, I sought him, but he could not be found.** *Mark the perfect man, and behold the upright: for the end of that man is peace. But the transgressors shall be destroyed together: the end of the wicked shall be cut off. But the salvation of the righteous is of the LORD: he is their strength in the time of trouble. And the LORD shall help them, and deliver them: he shall deliver them from the wicked, and save them, because they trust in him.* (Psalm 37:23-40 KJV)

God wants our whole hearts...

I know everything you have done, and you are not cold or hot. I wish you were either one or the other. But since you are **lukewarm and neither cold nor hot**, *I will spit you out of my mouth.* (Revelation 3:15-16 CEV)

ACCEPTANCE, APPROVAL & PEOPLE
PLEASING - WE ARE ALL BEING DELIVERED
FROM A "ROOT OF REJECTION"
12/4/2010

Success in the Kingdom has nothing to do with people we may or may not know or have connections with - it is simply in a humble and obedient heart that is turned towards Jesus as LORD, being Spirit led in ALL things, regardless of the approval or disapproval of men. We are only fit for the Kingdom if we are willing to forsake what others think of us in order to please the Lord.

God is dealing with all of mankind regarding different issues of the heart, in all different types of people. Right now many are going through a very dark period, especially in the last two or three weeks. Many have been really affected by what others think of them, myself included. God then revealed to me what was going on... The thing we need to keep in mind is **where is our FOCUS?** Is it on the Lord at ALL times? **When we start to FOCUS on other people or things we will start to 'feel' unstable and insecure.** The Lord is dealing with these **'roots of hindrance',** so His Spirit can flow through us and not be hindered - His Pure flow of LOVE... He wants to flood our whole heart with His Presence - if there are any 'roots of hindrance' left, He will have to get them out first. Work with Him on this and see the Salvation of the Lord! Yes, you can be totally FREE!!! The religious lie is that we will always be bound until we get to Heaven. But, whom the SON sets FREE is FREE IN 'DEED'. Do you understand what that means? A Deed is a Title. He has paid the price and holds the 'DEED' to your heart. When you receive Christ as your savior the enemy does not own you anymore. TURN your Focus to Christ and Him alone and ALL that hinders you will have to vacate the premises and fall off of you. Glory to God!!!

When we 'feel' that we need to have Acceptance, Approval or even realize that we have been 'People Pleasing', it is actually born out of a **'Root of Rejection'** that in turn causes us to get **into pride**. Fear of being rejected in any way means our FOCUS is off. It is important to remember that people do not reject you because of you, they reject you because of the way they see themselves and how they feel deep down about themselves and about God. They are actually crying out for help because they see something in you that they know is help for them, but pride causes them not to ask for help. They attack and reject because they 'feel' rejected by God and in some cases by you and in turn get into pride. God has shown me that the thing to do is just **GIVE LOVE and UNDERSTANDING** to them. **Someone has got to GIVE, it might as well be you! LOVE breaks the back of pride and when we Give Love, it will also FREE us from this root of rejection.** There is a **strategy** involved when God tells us to pray for and love our enemies. It Frees us and them at the same time! God is a multi-purpose God!

It all comes down to it not being about us at all, but always, in all things, it **ALL is always about HIM.** The Lord is always accepting, He is such a good God! I love Him! And I love ALL of you! God Bless!

Scripture References

Please read these scriptures - there is more revelation in them...

And it happened as they were going in the way, one said to Him, Lord, I will follow You wherever You go. And Jesus said to him, Foxes have holes, and birds of the air have nests, but the Son of Man has nowhere to lay His head. And He said to another, Follow Me! But he said, Lord, first allow me to go and bury my father. Jesus said to him, Let the dead bury their dead, but you go and proclaim the kingdom of God. And another also said, Lord, I will follow You, but first allow me to take leave of those in my house. And Jesus said to him, No one, having put his hand to the plow and looking back, is fit for the kingdom of God. (Luke 9:57-62 MKJV) **If we are worried about what others think about us then we are not fit for the Kingdom...**

You have heard that it was said, "You shall love your neighbor and hate your enemy." But I say to you, Love your enemies, bless those who curse you, do good to those who hate you, and pray for those who despitefully use you and persecute you, so that you may become Sons of your Father in Heaven (a 'Son' is someone who is not just a child, but has become 'perfect' or mature IN HIM). *For He makes His sun to rise on the evil and on the good, and sends rain on the just and on the unjust. For if you love those who love you, what reward do you have? Do not even the tax-collectors do the same? And if you greet your brothers only, what do you do more than others? Do not even the tax-collectors do so? Therefore be perfect, even as your Father in Heaven is perfect* (or mature). (Matthew 5:43-48 MKJV)

Sometimes it is your calling that 'Rejection' confirms in your life...

For Jesus himself testified, that a prophet hath no honour in his own country. (John 4:44 KJV)

The FEAR of Rejection keeps many from truly living at all...

A Word From The Lord For 2011, "I Hear The Sound Of My Justice & Judgment Reigning In 2011, This Is The Year Of The Prophetic & The Prophetic Will Declare War On The Spirit Of Religion, The Key To The House Of David Is Being Handed To The Next Generation - To My Watchmen"

5/10/2010, 7/7/2010, 12/6/2010, Released 12/11/2010

And the Lord said, **"Do you hear what I hear? I said, Do you hear what I hear? It is the Sound of My Mighty Rushing Winds of Change, bringing The Justice and Judgment that will Rein, Reign and Rain in the year 2011. This will make way for the fullness of the Apostolic to emerge and come to fruition by the year 2012. This Sound that can only be deciphered in the Spirit realm is the 'Changing of the Guard'. What you hear is the sound of Authority shifting hands and being wrought in this next Generation, the Generation of Many Five Fold Prophets, whom I have gifted with many diverse giftings. I AM is Changing the Guards and Passing the Reins of Authority in the Earth to My Watchmen. I AM is releasing My Watchmen to declare WAR on the spirit of religion** (Jezebel, poverty and the 'man spirit' or carnal mindset). **Do not expect Jezebel to give up without a fight. Your strategy is to simply Stand, Be Still and Know that I Am God, move only when I release you to do so and keep your heart consecrated to Me alone. I AM is coming to 'Collect'** (to bring things together or execute) **My 'New Covenant' in the earth. My Prophets will sense a heightening in their giftings as the New Year rings in, look for it and receive it, says the Lord of Hosts."** The fullness of the Apostolic will come to fruition by 2012, 12 being the number of the Apostolic - this has a significant meaning behind it. This is God's Government, Established and Resolute in the Earth, in its fullness.

I had a vision of a Giant Book. This Book represented the **TRUE BIBLE**, a Spiritual Bible, Untouched and Unchanged by man's hand. It was closed and positioned over the United States - in the

Heartland, over the State of Illinois (this could be because Illinois is considered the Apostolic State). It had a lock on it and it could only be seen by those who lived and walked in the Spirit. There was a Key that was there all along, but was hidden from us until a **certain time**. I believe this 'Key' represented the Key of the House of David. This 'certain time' was the time when the Spirit of the Lord would lead those, who live and walk in the Spirit, into **ALL TRUTH**. *However, when He, the Spirit of Truth, has come, He will guide you into All Truth. For He shall not speak of Himself, but whatever He hears, He shall speak. And He will announce to you things to come. He will glorify Me, for He will receive of Mine and will announce it to you. All things that the Father has are Mine. Therefore I said that He will take of Mine and will announce it to you.* (John 16:13-15 MKJV)

Everyone is waiting for a 'physical temple' to be rebuilt in the earth, in Israel. I believe that will happen in the natural, but also, God keeps calling America (the United States), His **'New Israel'.** He is rebuilding His temple metaphorically - the Key to the House of David is the access to His Holy temple being raised up In the hearts of the people in America, His **'New Israel'.** This is where it will begin, in the 'heartland'. Does this mean that people of other Nations will not be a part of it? No, it will just be more condensed and begin in The United States.

In the vision, I also saw the Lord hand this Key, to this **'True Bible',** to a certain group of people. They appeared to be dressed in worn and torn clothing. They were those that have been hidden away, those who have been hiding in their caves with the **'refiner's fire'** and those who have found the **'Secret Place'.** They are His Sons in whom He was well pleased (because their hearts have been turned towards Him, and, they are Spirit led in ALL things in ALL of life). These were people who didn't need fame, glory, or money to do what they do for the Lord. Just to know that they pleased the heart of God was enough for them. These people represented the **True Apostolic Authority in the Earth** (the word Apostolic refers to the anointing). **There are Apostolic Apostles, Apostolic Prophets, Apostolic Evangelists,**

Apostolic Pastors and Apostolic Teachers. The Apostolic Anointing refers to a high authority in the spirit realm, and it is also an **'ordering anointing'** - putting all things into the place or order that they were meant. When someone who has this anointing is in leadership, there is order and peace that follows.

And the Lord said, **"This new and 'unlikely' alliance is My True and Rightful Government. And, they will take the Authority in the Earth by Warring for it in the Spirit realm in 2011."** *And from the days of John the Baptist until now the kingdom of Heaven is taken by violence, and the violent take it by force.* (Matthew 11:12 MKJV) 'Violent' means intense passion and 'by force' means to literally snatch away - they will **'Take it'** (all in the spirit of Love of course, keeping our good fruit in tact - simply to advance and to keep moving forward).

God calls this Alliance, His **'House of Power in the Earth'.** This has to do with His GRACE - His **'House of Power'** is being birthed right now (notice the number of the scripture above, Matthew 11:12 - interesting, this is occurring in **2011** and into **2012**). And the Lord said, **"I will not put My anointing or blessing on anything that I did not initiate. Those in My 'House of Power' have an Understanding of Grace and they are walking in it with DOMINION - True Ambassadors of Christ in the Earth. The enemy can not tell the difference between these people who live and walk in the Spirit, and Christ, not only in the Spirit realm but also in the natural as well."** *And this is the will of Him who sent Me, that everyone who sees the Son and believes on Him should have everlasting life. And I will **Raise Him up at the last day.*** (John 6:40 MKJV)

*For unto us a child is born, unto us a **son is given: and the government shall be upon his shoulder:** and his name shall be called Wonderful, Counselor, The mighty God, The everlasting Father, The Prince of Peace. Of the **increase of his government and peace there shall be no end,** upon the **throne of David, and upon his kingdom, to ORDER it,*** (remember, the Apostolic is an 'ORDERING'

Anointing) *and to establish it with **judgment and with justice** from henceforth even for ever. The zeal of the LORD of hosts will perform this.* (Isaiah 9:6-7 KJV)

The Lord revealed to me that 2010 was the year of Judgment and Order being restored (this started in God's **True Church** first, we had to go through this refinement so we could go into 2011 prepared for war time). **2011 is the year of Warring and pulling down the stronghold of the spirit of religion, the poverty mindset and the man spirit - in the spirit of Joshua and Jeremiah. The Work of 2010 and 2011 will make way for the Fullness of the Apostolic to emerge in 2012.**

The Key to the House of David is found in the Secret Place. David's House is a House of Worship. True Worship involves TRUSTING in the Lord, FOCUSING on Christ and the Cross, and seeing Him as our Source for all things, not mammon (or idols). This is God's Restoration and Resurrection Power in the Earth.

The following scripture depicts the Falling of 'man's church system'. *See, O strong man* (a man in his own strength is in pride), *the Lord will send you violently away, gripping you with force, Twisting you round and round like a ball he will send you out into a wide country: there you will come to your end, and there will be the carriages of your pride, O shame of your lord's house!* ***And I will have you forced out of your place of authority, and pulled down from your position.*** *And in that day I will send for my servant, **Eliakim** (this name means 'God Rises'), the son of Hilkiah: And **I will put your robe on him, and put your band about him, and I will give your authority into his hand: and he will be a FATHER TO THE MEN OF JERUSALEM*** (True Fatherly Leadership is coming back to the Earth), *and to the family of Judah. And **I will give the Key of the family of David into his care; and what he keeps open will be shut by no one, and what he keeps shut no one will make open.*** *And I will put him like a nail in a safe place; and he will be for a seat of glory to his father's family. And all the glory of* *his father's family will be hanging on him, all their offspring, every small vessel, even the cups and the basins. In that day, says the Lord of armies, will the nail fixed in a safe place give way; and it will be cut down, and in its fall the weight hanging on it will be cut off, for the Lord has said it.* (Isaiah 22:17-25 BBE)

Remember, there are two different 'churches' of God. There is the **'established man's church system'**, built around the **love of money** and there is the **true church** - those who have received Grace, truly repented and put God first in their hearts and minds. There are many who are a part of the true church who are attending 'man's church system' (God has a purpose for them being there). How do we know them? Well, their fruit will tell. One way to identify this 'man spirit' is when we see God's word compromised, desperation and panhandling for money (they think they are their own provider or source, not God). Another way to tell is **Law** versus **GRACE**. The Gospel of Grace is Power Unto Salvation - True Salvation, the power of the Cross. I will discuss this in the Word called, **'THE GREAT AWAKENING HAS COME, THE VEIL OF RELIGION IS BEING LIFTED, "I AM WILL CLEAN YOUR HANDS AND RENEW YOUR MIND, REJOICE FOR YOUR REDEMPTION DRAWS NIGH" SALVATION IS HERE & NOW, WE ARE FREE'.**

I believe we are in the time of the church age of **Laodicea.** This is very evident if you look at the fruit. **Laodicea** is the seventh and **Final church** in scripture. God keeps reiterating this **'pride of man'** issue and He is saying judgment is coming to the religious man's church system and to the people of the world next. Remember, this judgment is not going to look like fire and brimstone (although it may 'feel' that way), it is simply a separation of pure from impure at a heart level. Judgment had to come to God's True Church first, this is the reason why it looked like the man's church system, and the world, were still prospering while the true people of God were suffering. Now, we will see God's people prosper as we see judgment coming to the man's church system and the world. These are all of **the elements of Judgment, Justice, and Reigning, just like King**

David brought. *And David reigned over all Israel. And David did judgment and justice to all his people.* (2 Samuel 8:15 MKJV) *And David reigned over all Israel, and did judgment and justice among all his people.* (1 Chronicles 18:14 MKJV)

Let us investigate what **Laodicea** means in comparison with the church today. Laodicea means **'uncommitted'.** In Revelation chapter 3, the Bible talks about the church of **Laodicea** as being **lukewarm (apathetic, indifferent).** In the ancient Greek, this word means **'justice of the people',** or **'man's justice'.** This would be man taking justice into his own hands or trying to justify himself based on his performance of the law - this is legalism and religion. **Laos** means people or man. **Dicea** means **'opinions' or 'judgment'.** We all know that man's judgment and opinions are not always in line with the Truth of the Word of God. The Lord revealed to me that there are **three different meanings** to how this can be taken and they would all be correct.

The first is in religion - man forming an **'opinion'** or establishing a belief based on one's own experiences, misjudgments and misinterpretation of the Bible. Many who are trapped in this way of thinking are convinced that they know what is best and right. They are very legalistic and have not sought God to acknowledge Him in any of their ways, so their path is a crooked one, but they cannot see it because they are **blinded by pride.** *God has sent them strong delusion because they didn't love the truth* (2 Thessalonians 2:11 paraphrased). **The second is in wrong judgment of man -** misjudging or making a snap judgment based on appearance or prejudice, pride and hatred. In this case our Focus is way off. We should be Focused on the Lord and not each other. This is NOT Love, it is hate. Many of the above mentioned are a part of **'man's church system'.** And **thirdly - man being judged by God,** the separation of the wheat from the tares - read Matthew 13.

This **'man spirit'** that has taken over the man's church system of today and has formed many different sects of Religion based on **man's opinion and comfort -** all of it is **built around the love of money** (money is the focus or is attached to most things that happen there). Our Source is what or who we focus on to meet our needs, this is also what we **Love** and **Worship.** Whatever our Focus is on, that same thing becomes our 'god'. If it is any 'god' besides Jehovah, it is considered **idolatry.** We cannot serve God and mammon (mammon can be money, or any other thing we make our source besides God alone). This is why **it is impossible for those who love money, to truly love others.** Serving God and living under Grace requires us to Love God and Love Others. If we are serving money, we cannot serve God. If we are serving money then we are Not His and we do not hear His voice - His Sheep know His voice and ARE Spirit led in ALL of life. *For the love of money is a root of all evils, of which some having lusted after, they were seduced from the faith and pierced themselves through with many sorrows.* (1 Timothy 6:10 MKJV) *No one can serve two masters. For either he will hate the one and love the other, or else he will hold to the one and despise the other. You cannot serve God and mammon.* (Matthew 6:24 MKJV)

*And to the angel of the church of the **Laodicea** write: The Amen, the faithful and true Witness, the Head of the creation of God, says these things: I know your works, that **you are neither cold nor hot.** I would that you were cold or hot. So because you are **lukewarm,** and neither cold nor hot, I will **vomit you out of My mouth.** Because you say, I am rich and increased with goods and have need of nothing, and do not know that you are wretched and miserable and poor and blind and naked, I counsel you to buy from Me gold purified by fire* (put your hope on Me), *so that you may be rich; and white clothing, so that you may be clothed, and so that the shame of your nakedness does not appear. And anoint your eyes with eye salve, so that you may **SEE.** As many as I love, I rebuke and chasten; therefore be zealous and repent. Behold, I stand at the door and knock. If anyone hears My voice and opens the door, I will come in to him and will dine with him and he with Me. To him who overcomes I will grant to sit with Me in My throne, even as I also overcame and have sat down with My Father in His throne. He who has an ear, let him hear* (he who is humble enough to hear and receive) *what the Spirit says to the churches.* (Revelation 3:14-22 MKJV)

For I want you to know what a **great conflict** *I have for you and those at* **Laodicea,** *and for as many as have not seen my face in the flesh, that their hearts might be comforted, being knit together in love, and to all riches of the full assurance of the understanding, to the full knowledge of the mystery of God, and of the Father, and of Christ; in whom are hidden all the treasures of wisdom and knowledge. And I say this that not anyone should beguile you with enticing words. For though I am absent in the flesh, yet I am with you in the spirit, rejoicing and beholding your order and the steadfastness of your* **faith in Christ**. *Therefore as you have received Christ Jesus the Lord, so walk in Him, rooted and built up in Him, and established in the faith, as you have been taught, abounding in it with thanksgiving.* **Beware lest anyone rob you through philosophy and vain deceit, according to the 'tradition of men', according to the 'elements of the world', and not according to Christ.** *For* **in Him dwells all the fullness** *of the Godhead bodily. And you* **ARE complete in Him,** *who is the Head of all principality and power, in whom also you are circumcised with the circumcision made without hands, in putting off the body of the sins of the flesh by the circumcision of Christ, buried with Him in baptism, in whom also you were raised through the faith of the working of God, raising Him from the dead. And you, being dead in your sins and the uncircumcision of your flesh, He has made alive together with Him, having forgiven you all trespasses, blotting out the handwriting of ordinances that was against us, which was contrary to us, and has taken it out of the way, nailing it to the cross. Having stripped rulers and authorities, He made a show of them publicly, triumphing over them in it.* **Therefore let no one (man) judge you in food or in drink, or in respect of a feast, or of the new moon, or of the sabbaths.** *For these are a shadow of things to come, but the body is of Christ. Let no one defraud you, delighting in humility and worship of the angels, intruding into things which he has not seen, without a cause being* **vainly puffed up** *by his fleshly mind, and not holding the Head, from whom all the body, having been supplied through the joints and bands, and having been joined together, will grow with the growth of God.* **If then you died with Christ from the elements of the world, why, as though living in the world, are** *you subject to its ordinances: touch not, taste not, handle not; which things are all for corruption in the using, according to the commands and Doctrines of men? These things indeed have a reputation of wisdom in **self-imposed worship and humility**, and unsparing severity of the body, but are **not of any value** for the satisfying of the flesh.* (Colossians 2:1-23 MKJV) *Such things sound impressive if said in a deep enough voice. They even **give the illusion of being pious and humble and ascetic**. But they're just another way of showing off, making yourselves **look** important.* (Colossians 2:23 *THE MESSAGE*) **False humility is still pride, in disguise.**

The Lord was also revealing something to me about the **'mark of the beast'.** Besides the 'physical' mark that would be on the forehead and the hand, the Lord was showing me that it has a figurative or spiritual meaning behind it as well. He told me that **Pride is the 'mark' of a false prophet.** Then He showed me that **pride is a 'headstrong' spirit,** hence the 'mark' on the forehead. Then there is the 'mark' on the hand - **'The work of our hands'.** When we do not see God as our source, then we get into fear about our needs being met so we become **our own source** and go to **work based on fear** and **disregard obedience** to God in this area, therefore we **make ourselves our own god.** This is also a form of pride, hence the 'mark' on the hand. The Lord showed me that the number 6 is the number of man and 666 is the 'trinity of man' (when man's mind, will and emotions becomes his own 'source' or 'god'). *"I, the LORD, refuse to accept anyone who is **proud**. Only those who **LIVE BY FAITH** are acceptable to me."* (Habakkuk 2:4 CEV) Pride makes man the 'sons of the enemy' and Humility makes man the 'Sons of God'. Does this mean that 'work' is wrong? No, God just wants us to acknowledge Him and ask Him what He wants us to do with our lives - this is where His blessing lies. It may be, in having a 'job', but did we ask Him first?

And the Lord said, **"ARISE WOMEN OF VALOR!" There is a Remnant of Women that God is raising up in the spirit of Esther and Deborah, to be authorities in the earth and they will bring the Zoe anointing - bringing the life of God, getting** the ball rolling so to speak. **This is not necessarily pertaining to Government in man's sense of the word, but in God's Government. His Government is unseen, but it will be recognized.**

The Lord gave me this scripture, Isaiah 11:11 - notice the number again, **11**. This is what that scripture says and what He revealed to me about it and He said to Expect to be **Warring for Freedom for, and then ultimately being FREE from these things listed below, in 2011...**

And it shall be in that day, the Lord shall again set His hand, the second time, to recover the remnant of His people that remains,...

From Assyria - Assyria represents Oppression coming from people who are not the rightful authority. See Isaiah 52:4, Hosea 5:13 and Hosea 11:5.

And from Egypt, - Egypt represents Jezebel and the spirit of religion. This also represents slavery, a worldly system of compromise, slavery to mammon and the poverty mentality or **'Children of Israel mentality'.** Egypt also represents false Glory and heavy Labor - meaning things will be easier when we finally Trust the Lord to be our Source. See Jeremiah 34:13, Isaiah 20:5 and Isaiah 45:14.

And from Pathros, - Pathros (Python and Ahab) represents the 'heads' of authority that are 'people pleasing' and being controlled by those under their authority. Pathos also represents the spirit of rebellion and worship to Jezebel (who turns them on to other gods including Manipulation, Emotions swaying the mind, enticement, deceit, persuasion, and that which causes the land to be desolate). See Jeremiah 44:15, 17 and Ezekiel 30:14.

And from Ethiopia, - Ethiopia represents man worshiping other men and prostituting ourselves based on 'merchandising'. This symbolizes the 'man spirit' that is worshiped and made a false idol. This will be exposed and will fall. We will not be ashamed or confounded by man anymore, but the confusion and confoundedness will be turned around on the perpetrator. Rejection will not have any effect or sting, because we will find and have our Identity and Hope in Christ - nothing can discourage or disappoint us. The truth will make the crooked places straight and many who claim to be atheists will turn and worship the one true God Jehovah. See Isaiah 45:14-19.

And from Persia, - Persia actually represents the positive effect that **Justice** and **Judgment** brings (the result is the freedom). **Order will be restored and Peace will be a result of it.** Women will be freed from discrimination, especially in the Church. Many women will be promoted by GOD to high places of authority. See the Book of Ester, Judges 4:4, Galatians 3:26-29, Nehemiah 2:6 and Ezra 7:11-26.

And from Shinar, - Shinar represents the Unity of man with arrogance against God (This is where the Tower of Babel was being built). God said that when man is in unity nothing will be impossible to him. This will also bring on the second coming of Christ. Social Networking is making unity more possible now than ever before. See Genesis 10:8-10 and Genesis 11:1-9.

And from Hamath, - Hamath represents a seed of confusion. Many aspects of Python are also represented by Hamath. In Isaiah 10:9, Hamath is described as being 'like' Arpad. Arpad means 'seed'. *Concerning Damascus. Hamath is confounded, and Arpad: for they have heard evil tidings: they are fainthearted; there is sorrow on the sea; it cannot be quiet.* (Jeremiah 49:23 KJV) The Lord is delivering His people from the 'seed of confusion' and from faintheartedness, sorrow and complacency.

And from the coasts of the sea. (Isaiah 11:11 MKJV)

Scripture References

*So let him who thinks he stands take heed lest he fall. No temptation has taken you but what is common to man; but God is faithful, who will not allow you to be tempted above what you are able, but with the temptation also will make a way to escape, so that you may be able to bear it. Therefore, my dearly beloved, **flee from idolatry**.* (1 Corinthians 10:12-14 MKJV)

Trust in Jehovah with all your heart, and lean not to your own understanding. In all your ways acknowledge Him, and He shall direct your paths. (Proverbs 3:5-6 MKJV)

And seven priests shall bear seven trumpets of ram's horns in front of the ark. And the seventh day you shall go around the city seven times, and the priests shall blow with the trumpets. And it shall be when they make a long blast with the ram's horn, and when you hear the sound of the trumpet, all the people shall shout with a great shout. And the wall of the city shall fall down flat, and the people shall go up, each man straight before him. And Joshua the son of Nun called the priests and said to them, Take up the ark of the covenant, and let seven priests carry seven ram's horns in front of the ark of Jehovah. (Joshua 6:4-6 MKJV)

But Jehovah said to me, Do not say, I am a boy; for you shall go to all that I shall send you, and whatever I command you, you shall speak. Do not be afraid of their faces; for I am with you to deliver you, says Jehovah. And Jehovah put forth His hand, and touched my mouth. And Jehovah said to me, Behold, I have put My Words in your mouth. Behold! I have this day set you over the nations and over the kingdoms, to root out, and to pull down, and to destroy, and to throw down, to build, and to plant. And the Word of Jehovah came to me, saying, Jeremiah, what do you see? And I said, I see a rod of an almond tree.

And Jehovah said to me, You have seen well; for I will watch over My Word to perform it. (Jeremiah 1:7-12 MKJV)

For sin shall not have dominion over you: ***for ye are not under the law, but under grace.*** (Romans 6:14 KJV)

Consider what I say, and the Lord will give you understanding in all things. Remember that ***Jesus Christ of the seed of David*** *was raised from the dead according to my gospel, in which I suffer ill as an evildoer, even to bonds. But the Word of God is not chained. Therefore I endure all things for the sake of the elect, that they may also obtain the salvation which is in Christ Jesus with eternal glory. For faithful is the Word, for if we died with Him, we shall also live with Him.* (2 Timothy 2:7-11 MKJV)

And by your sword you shall live, and shall serve your brother. And it shall be when you shall have the **DOMINION,** *you shall break his yoke from off your neck.* (Genesis 27:40 MKJV) Also, note what the CEV version says, interesting... *You will live by the power of your sword and be your brother's slave. But* ***when you DECIDE TO BE FREE, you will break loose.*** (Genesis 27:40 CEV)

And the righteous shall see, and fear, and shall laugh at him, saying, Behold, the man who did not make God his strength, but trusted in the abundance of his riches, he was strong in his wickedness. But I am like a green olive tree in the house of God; I trust in the mercy of God forever and ever. (Psalms 52:6-8 KJV)

"THE LAST SHALL BE FIRST & THE FIRST SHALL BE LAST, I AM RESHAPING YOUR PAST & CHANGING YOUR TESTIMONY, WITH PHYSICAL HEAT, I WILL ERADICATE POVERTY"

4/24/2008, Released 11/2/2010

I heard the Lord say, **"The last shall be the first and the first shall be the last. I will be taking My people back, back from the agonizing vice grip that has been placed on their hearts and I will also be taking them back into their beginnings. I have to cause them to deal with the hurtful things, and I have to heal their beginnings before I can take them into the next season where I will Modernize and Convert them into Trailblazers - Pioneers for the future and into their Potential, into their Hope and into their Destiny."**

The body of Christ is now coming into a season of total reliance and Trust in the Lord. A **'Blind Faith'** kind of Trust, where we cannot see the next steps in front of us, but we have only to rely on His voice and His hand to gently nudge, guide and lead us. **Do Not get ahead of God.** He is teaching us by His Spirit to respect His ORDER of Authority. This respect for His Order of Authority is the ABILITY for functionality in the Body - it is what allows the Flow of the anointing. Then we can be in Alignment, so the flow can happen unhindered. The Order is this… *He that descended is the same also that ascended up far above all heavens, that he might fill all things.) And he gave some, **Apostles**; and some, **Prophets**; and some, **Evangelists**; and some, **Pastors** and **Teachers**; For the perfecting of the saints, for the work of the ministry, for the edifying of the body of Christ:* (Ephesians 4:10-12 KJV)

In this Alignment is the Grace and POWER of God that will now be more tangible than ever before to people who have and haven't had the Lord use them in the Supernatural. This POWER will become more INTENSE and HOT than you have ever physically felt before. We will begin to see manifestations of miracles. NEW Revelation will be coming like Manna from Heaven. And the Lord said, **"Do not fear the Heat. In this Heat I will be healing your physical ailments and with this HEAT, and by FIRE, I will Realign All Things - especially your innards. These are things that have been askew for some time now and My people have learned to just live with it, but no more! They will finally have relief, not only in body and soul, but also the Spirit of Poverty will be dealt with."** The Lord gave me a clear revelation about the spirit of poverty and how it begins in the stomach. This spirit is always afraid of not having. The first physical manifestation of this fear is when people are hungry they begin to get into fear about the Lord supplying their needs. This physical Heat that He talks about is going to Eradicate the spirit of poverty, and the Lord said, **"Starve it out with Fasting."**

I hear the Lord saying, **"Unusual Miracles and Manifestations will begin to take place. Just because you haven't seen it done this way or that way before does not mean that it is not God. Do not judge ANY move of My Spirit, or you will be left out of it. Let Me out of the box and I will show you great and mighty things that you know not of. I will, through the revelation of Total Trust in ME, Renovate, Repair, Restore, Mend, Fix Up, and Refurbish you, for this 'NOW FAITH' season is upon you. For NOW FAITH is 'Substant', NOW! It is NOW FAITH! Get a hold of the fact that it is NOW. Stop believing for somewhere down the road when the river rises and the cattle come home! Your Miracle IS NOW and already exists on the inside of you. It is what My Kingdom is made up of and it wants to be let out! Believe it and you shall see it. When I give the command to you, to pray or to minister, this is the only time that you should step out. BE Spirit Led only. At this time, I need you to reach into the third heaven and 'pull' your miracles into your midst. It has been there all along, you just couldn't SEE it until this NOW Faith Season, for MY Ways are not your ways and My Thoughts are not your thoughts. My Realm is not subject to your realm, for your realm contains the five limited dimensions of Length, Width, Height, Space and Time. Where I am taking you there are NO dimensions - it is FREE and** undeniably everywhere and every time. Open your minds up, and you will SEE the Manifestation of MY GLORY. You will see the manifestation begin to take place everywhere your eyes can see and can not see. Harvest is springing up - I said harvest is springing up - get your sickle and harvest it, harvest it! Begin to work your fields. For like an Onion, I am pealing back the Years and the Layers of your wounded remembrance. These repressed memories will come to you in dreams, visions, visitations and in some cases out of body experiences. Do not say, 'This is the enemy', and Fear Not, for I am with you. I was there with you when these things took place. Have I not said, 'I knew you before the foundations of the earth'? Have I not said, 'I will never leave you nor forsake you'? For in this season I am Reshaping your past and Changing your testimony. Like a renegade, you will do an about face and turn from the hurts of your past. You will no longer look back at the past with hurt in your heart, but with Compassion and Understanding for those who have perpetrated against you and forgiveness will come, forgiveness will come, forgiveness will come. Forgiveness for the perpetrator, forgiveness for your self and forgiveness for ME, says God. These things that were hurtful from the past are Roots of Hindrances and they will be revealed and unveiled to you. Do not run for fear, but STAND and confront, and you will see the enemy that you have feared, even since your childhood, dissipate before your very eyes. You will say, 'it is over, it is finally over'! When this step by step process is complete, you will be complete, nothing missing nothing broken, whole in every way and in every area - Shalom. You will be cleansed and healed of the past and you will not say 'I have no past', you will say, 'My past was a gift that was FOR ME, something that made me beautiful, something that I can now glean Knowledge and the Understanding from and be able to help others be Over comers as I am an Over comer'. The healing doesn't come when you just deny that the past ever happened. The healing comes when it is confronted and when I am allowed to heal every part of your hearts and every part of your souls. If My people constantly focus on the past, they will never be able to SEE the future."

Our destiny is waiting, so let us press toward the mark for the prize of the high calling of God in Christ Jesus, and don't let anything ever stand in your way. And the Lord said, **"NOW is the time, for your future is NOW and NOW is your time to Overcome, says the Lord of Hosts."**

The Lord told me that we are going to be able to see the **'red'** on people in areas where they need healing. Like infrared can pick up heat, this is where to apply the **'heat'**. When we see this, it is the time that we are to step out and pray for their healing.

Scripture References

So the last shall be first, and the first last: for many be called, but few chosen. (Matthew 20:16 KJV)

To whom God would make known what is the riches of the glory of this mystery among the Gentiles; which is Christ in you, the hope of glory: (Colossians 1:27 KJV)

The centurion answered and said, Lord, I am not worthy that thou shouldest come under my roof: but speak the word only, and my servant shall be healed. For I am a man under authority, having soldiers under me: and I say to this man, Go, and he goeth; and to another, Come, and he cometh; and to my servant, Do this, and he doeth it. When Jesus heard it, he marveled, and said to them that followed, Verily I say unto you, I have not found so great faith, no, not in Israel. And I say unto you, That many shall come from the east and west, and shall sit down with Abraham, and Isaac, and Jacob, in the kingdom of heaven. But the children of the kingdom shall be cast out into outer darkness: there shall be weeping and gnashing of teeth. And Jesus said unto the centurion, Go thy way; and as thou hast believed, so be it done unto thee. And his servant was healed in the selfsame hour. (Matthew 8:8-13 KJV)

He that loveth me not keepeth not my sayings: and the word which ye hear is not mine, but the Father's which sent me. These things have I spoken unto you, being yet present with you. But the Comforter, which is the Holy Ghost, whom the Father will send in my name, he shall teach you all things, and bring all things to your remembrance, whatsoever I have said unto you. Peace I leave with you, my peace I give unto you: not as the world giveth, give I unto you. Let not your heart be troubled, neither let it be afraid. (John 14:24-27 KJV)

Now we have received, not the spirit of the world, but the spirit which is of God; that we might know the things that are freely given to us of God. Which things also we speak, not in the words which man's wisdom teacheth, but which the Holy Ghost teacheth; comparing spiritual things with spiritual. But the natural man receiveth not the things of the Spirit of God: for they are foolishness unto him: neither can he know them, because they are spiritually discerned. (1 Corinthians 2:12-14 KJV)

Now faith is the substance of things hoped for, the evidence of things not seen. (Hebrews 11:1 KJV)

The fundamental fact of existence is that this trust in God, this faith, is the firm foundation under everything that makes life worth living. It's our handle on what we can't see. (Hebrews 11:1 **THE MESSAGE**)

THE LORD IS ABOUT TO USE US TO SOW 'PROVOKING' SEEDS OF TRUTH, I AM IS DECLARING WAR ON THE SPIRIT OF RELIGION, REVIVAL IS HERE & NOW, I WILL RESTORE THE KEY OF THE HOUSE OF DAVID, JUDAH, GO & TAKE YOUR LAND!

5/19/2008, Released 1/20/2011

The Lord **NEVER** ceases to amaze me. In so many things, in so many ways He confirms Himself to me and boggles my mind on a regular basis. There is NO being bored with the Lord! I love Him so much! I had not read or even looked at this Word, since He gave it to me in May of 2008. To be honest, it kind of took me back a little, when I realized that it was saying a lot of what was in the 2011 Word. I had actually forgotten all of this Word except the 'Provoking seeds' part. The Lord was pressing on me to go and find this Word and release it. So, here it is. Lord, I pray that as Your people read this Word, a fresh anointing and a Deeper Understanding fall on all who read it. ALL Glory to You, Father always in ALL things, in Jesus Name, amen.

The Lord is about to use us to sow **'Provoking Seeds of Truth'** into the hearts of **ALL** types of people. This seed will be an **APPEAL** for their Heart to **'Stir Something Up'** on the inside of them and Challenge their Hearts and Spirits to **ACTION**. And the Lord said, **"I will be using My Prophets and the like, to sow these seeds of 'provoke' into each other and into other people's hearts."** This will be challenging the religious spirits and mindsets that many people have had in their lives - even the unsaved have these spirits and mindsets. Many who think they are saved are not saved. And the Lord said, **"With this obedience, I will DECLARE WAR on the spirit of religion, on religious strongholds and bring FREEDOM to My Body. This will also put a pull on the hearts of believers, and unbelievers alike to question why they believe what it is that they believe. The TRUTH will bear witness with their spirits. I will put a Curiosity and a Hunger in their hearts to search out Truth, The TRUTH OF MY WORD, says the Lord of Hosts."**

Then Jesus said to the Jews who believed on Him, If you **continue in My Word,** *you are My disciples indeed. And you shall* **know the truth, and the truth shall make you FREE.** *They answered Him, We are Abraham's seed and were never in bondage to anyone. How do you say, You will be made free? Jesus answered them, Truly, truly, I say to you,* **Whoever practices sin is the slave of sin.** *And the slave does not abide in the house forever, but the* **Son abides forever.** *Therefore if the Son* (Christ) *shall make you free, you shall be free indeed. I know that you are Abraham's seed, but you seek to kill Me because My Word has no place in you.* (John 8:31-37 MKJV) Leave it to the 'religious crowd' to misunderstand and not really SEE that Jesus was talking about being bound in their 'soulish' realm.

This seed is going to feel like **'casting your pearls before swine'.** Do not worry and **DO NOT question God.** Just do what God tells you to do (**IN ALL HUMILITY AND IN LOVE**), and when He tells you to do it and He will take care of the rest. This is where the **'people pleasing'** thing will have to go - straight out the window. We must do what God is telling us and when He tells us to do it and **TRUST HIM** with all things and with all people, even if you think this might make you look bad. Do not worry - you will not be ruining your testimony. And the Lord said, **"My Grace has got you covered, in fact, I will cause them to be 'attracted' to you at a future time."**

An example of this is when you tell someone about the supernatural aspects of God and they look at you like a **'deer seeing headlights'** and say, "Well, I've always been this religion and I want to just stick with what I'm 'comfortable' with and what I was brought up with." Just smile and **leave them with the seed, IN LOVE** - as awkward as it may be. Just because someone may not receive something you have said to them right then and there, does not mean that the seed was not sown in their heart. Do not argue religious points with them, this would just be a waste of time. He wants us to simply sow the seed and move on - **always in the Spirit of LOVE.** *But avoid foolish and unlearned questions, knowing that they give birth to strifes. But the servant of the Lord must not strive, but to be gentle to all, apt to teach,*

patient, in meekness instructing those who oppose, if perhaps God will
give them repentance to the acknowledging of the truth, and that they
awake out of the snare of the Devil, *having been taken captive by*
him, so as to do the will of that one. (2 Timothy 2:23-26 MKJV)

And the Lord said, **"I AM will be putting My Warriors in place,
as on a Chess Board. I will be strategically placing My Army of
Conduits in their rightful places of Authority and like a flood,
I will usher My power in. You will know where I AM and
where I am NOT. After My Great Army is in position, they
will receive My Power - Power with FIRE, My 'New Fire' and
My Glory will Reign in the earth, such as the world has never
seen before this time. I will be bringing a 'certain type of
destruction' to the United States."** When I see this in the spirit,
it looks like a giant tidal wave, but the Lord showed me that it is
a **'figurative wave'.** And the Lord said, **"When this giant wave
of Calamity hits, people who have been putting their Trust in
anything besides Me, will be in such fear that they will
Clamor to find the people who have sown these, 'difficult
provoking' seeds of Truth into their lives at an earlier time.
The 'sowers' will be brought back to their remembrance, and
they will search out, who it was that told them about the Truth
of My Word. They will see you as a link to the only way out,
like a raging river that has no where else to flow but through a
tiny 'channel'. I am about to make you a 'channel' for My
POWER and My LOVE to ignite this FIRE in their hearts. It
will start out small like a kindling fire** (stirring up of emotion)
**but, do not despise the 'small beginnings' that this seems to
be. My Revival Fire will then ignite and overtake this Great
Nation of AMERICA - My 'New Israel', this FRESH
Generation of young and old, for Revival is HERE and NOW,
Revival is HERE and NOW, Revival is NOW and I will do it
for My Namesake and My Glory, says the Lord of Hosts."**

Then the Lord said, **"I AM is Restoring The Key of the House
of David."** The Lord led me to some scriptures about the **Key of
the House of David** and what follows is what I found.

And it shall come to pass in that day, that I will call my servant Eliakim (this name means One whom God will raise up, or God rises) *the son of Hilkiah: And I will clothe him with thy robe* (This robe symbolizes a mantle of Authority and the Anointing), *and strengthen him with thy girdle* (this means restraint, this is how He strengthens us, in humility - pain is the process of power), *and I will commit* (entrust, hand over, assign, obligate) *thy government* (authority, administration, direction, command) *into his hand: and he shall be a father to the inhabitants of Jerusalem* (the holy city of Judah and possession of peace - the absence of pride brings peace), *and to the house of Judah* (meaning praise). **And the Key of the House of David will I lay upon his shoulder; so he shall open, and none shall shut; and he shall shut, and none shall open.** (Isaiah 22:20-22 KJV)

For unto us a child is born, unto us a Son is given: and the Government shall be upon his shoulder: and his name shall be called Wonderful, Counselor, The mighty God, The everlasting Father, The Prince of Peace. **Of the increase of his government and peace there shall be no end,** *upon the* **throne of David, and upon his kingdom, to order it,** *and to establish it with* **judgment and with justice** *from henceforth even for ever. The zeal of the LORD of hosts will perform this.* (Isaiah 9:6-7 KJV)

The Lord is talking about His Prophetic Army that will begin to take their rightful place of Authority under **Jesus' direct Authority** to be the **'True Authority In The Earth'.** And the Lord said, **"For many of you have hit the ceiling of where your authority is willing to go in ME. I will remove you from the authority's rule that is stagnant. You see, you can only go as far as your authority is willing to take you - IN ME. I will place you in position to Overtake the Land. Take the Land, Take the Land, JUDAH go and take Your Land! I The Lord Your God Will Help You Take It."** The Lord revealed to me that He is speaking of Spiritual authority here. He will also deal with other authorities, but in this particular instance it is Spiritual. He then said, **"I AM is Restoring My House of TRUE WORSHIP. For** you were created for Worship and My worshipers will worship me in Spirit and in Truth, says the Lord of Hosts."

"I, the Lord, will return and rebuild David's fallen house. I will build it from its ruins and set it up again." (Acts 15:16 CEV)

"Judah!" the LORD answered. "I'll help them take the land." (Judges 1:2 CEV)

If you have ears, listen to what the Spirit says to the churches. This is what you must write to the angel of the church in Philadelphia: I am the one who is holy and true, and I have the keys that belonged to David. When I open a door, no one can close it. And when I close a door, no one can open it. Listen to what I say. I know everything you have done. And I have placed before you an open door that no one can close. You were not very strong, but you obeyed my message and did not deny that you are my followers. Now you will see what I will do with those people who belong to **Satan's group.** *They claim to be Jews, but they are liars. I will make them come and kneel down at your feet. Then they will know that I love you.* (Revelation 3:6-8 CEV)

We do not want to be a part of 'Satan's group'. We want to be a Son of the Most High God. What distinguishes us? Are we rebellious and prideful? Or, are we humble, in alignment and in order? Do we let other 'gods', like money, people or things, order the steps we take? Or, are we ordered by God alone, by being Spirit led in all things and all of our ways? These are questions we will have to answer very soon.

Scripture References

And he said unto me, My grace is sufficient for thee: for my strength is made perfect in weakness. Most gladly therefore will I rather glory in my infirmities, that the power of Christ may rest upon me. (2 Corinthians 12:9 KJV) *Yes, I am glad to be weak or insulted or mistreated or to have troubles and sufferings, if it is for Christ. Because when I am weak, I am strong.* (2 Corinthians 12:10 CEV)

Go in through the narrow gate, for wide is the gate and broad is the way that leads to destruction, and many there are who go in through it. Because narrow is the gate and constricted is the way which leads to life, and there are few who find it. (Matthew 7:13-14 MKJV)

Speak to the sons of Israel and say to them, When you have passed over Jordan into the land of Canaan, then you shall drive out all those who live in the land from before you, and destroy all their carved images, and destroy all their molded images and pluck down all their high places. And you shall possess the land, and live in it. For I have given you the land to possess it. (Numbers 33:51-53 MKJV)

And he began to say unto them, This day is this scripture fulfilled in your ears. And all bare him witness, and wondered at the gracious words which proceeded out of his mouth. And they said, Is not this Joseph's son? And he said unto them, Ye will surely say unto me this proverb, Physician, heal thyself: whatsoever we have heard done in Capernaum, do also here in thy country. And he said, Verily I say unto you, No prophet is accepted in his own country. (Luke 4:21-24 KJV)

The Spirit shows what is true and will come and guide you into the full truth. The Spirit doesn't speak on his own. He will tell you only what he has heard from me, and he will let you know what is going to happen. (John 16:13 CEV)

We belong to God, and everyone who knows God will listen to us. But the people who don't know God won't listen to us. That is how we can tell the Spirit that speaks the truth from the one that tells lies. My dear friends, we must love each other. Love comes from God, and when we love each other, it shows that we have been given new life. We are now God's children, and we know him. (1 John 4:6-7 CEV)

This is he that came by water and blood, even Jesus Christ; not by water only, but by water and blood. And it is the Spirit that beareth witness, because the Spirit is truth. (1 John 5:6 KJV)

Seeing ye have purified your souls in obeying the truth through the Spirit unto unfeigned love of the brethren, see that ye love one another with a pure heart fervently: (1 Peter 1:22 KJV)

But the hour is coming, and now is, when the true worshipers shall worship the Father in spirit and truth, for the Father seeks such to worship Him. God is a spirit, and they who worship Him must worship in spirit and in truth. (John 4:23-24 MKJV)

GOD IS DEALING A STRATEGIC OFFENSIVE BLOW TO THE SPIRIT OF RELIGION, "STARVE IT OUT WITH PRAYER AND FASTING"

1/25/2011

Father, I pray that the **Spirit of Wisdom, Revelation, Truth and Understanding** sweep the Land and the blinders be taken off of the eyes of our hearts so we can SEE and Understand what Your Spirit is saying to Your people through this Word, in Jesus Name, amen.

God is calling many to fasting and praying. He has been revealing to me that there is a strong spirit of **UNBELIEF** in the land. It is what caused Jesus to not be able to do mighty works in His own land - **it was because of their unbelief.** Many of you are going to be **called to prayer and fasting - ESPECIALLY WHEN YOU ARE GOING TO MINISTER OR BE IN INTERCESSORY PRAYER.**

*Then His disciples understood that He spoke to them about John the Baptist. And when they came to the crowd, a man came to Him, kneeling down to Him and saying, Lord, have mercy on my son, for **he is a lunatic** (there is a link between depression, mental illness and the spirit of unbelief, I will talk about this later) and grievously vexed; for oftentimes he falls into the fire, and often into the water. And I brought him to Your disciples, and **they could not cure him.** Then Jesus answered and said, O **faithless and perverse generation,** how long shall I be with you? How long shall I suffer you? Bring him here to Me. And Jesus rebuked the demon, and he departed out of him. And the child was cured from that very hour. Then the disciples came to Jesus apart, and said, **Why could we NOT cast him out?** And Jesus said to them, **Because of your UNBELIEF.** For truly I say to you, **If you have faith like a grain of mustard seed,** you shall say to this mountain, Move from here to there. And it shall move. And **NOTHING shall be impossible to you. However, this kind does not go out except by Prayer and Fasting.*** (Matthew 17:13-21 MKJV)

165

When we go into battle, part of our **preparation should be to fast and pray**. This is so we are clear of the spirit of Unbelief that is **ROOTED IN PRIDE**. If we go to lay hands on someone to pray for their healing and we have any Pride or the spirit of Unbelief, it will do us no good - like the Disciples in the above scripture. Jesus said, *"However, this kind does not go out except by prayer and fasting."* (Matthew 17:21 MKJV) This will also help us be able to confront any Unbelief that the person being prayed for may have.

The Key to be FREE from Pride and Unbelief is Fasting and Praying, if we allow God to lead us through it and stay in obedience to His Voice... We also need to allow it to take us to **TRUE HUMILITY.** You see, it is our **FLESH that doesn't believe.** Our Spirit does believe. If we crucify the flesh the spirit of Unbelief will also go. If we think there is no possible way we could be affected by this spirit then we are **IN PRIDE** and **UNBELIEF.**

There is a link between Unbelief and Disobedience. How can people walk in Grace and be Spirit led (Truly Be Saved) if they do not believe? Before we can have a True Revival we must Fast this spirit of Pride and Unbelief out of the land!!!

Depression, mental illness and the like are **'minions' of Pride and Unbelief.** Python is the Principality that is responsible for anything that ails us that has to do with the **head, the neck, the spine, the lungs and the stomach. The Root is Pride and Unbelief.** Look at the scripture below...

*And immediately the **FATHER** of the **CHILD** cried out and said with tears, Lord, I believe. **Help my UNBELIEF.*** (This was generational and it was passed to the child) *And seeing that a crowd is running together, Jesus rebuked the unclean spirit, saying to him, **Dumb and deaf spirit*** (the dumb and deaf spirits are minions of Unbelief - having to do with the head), *I command you, come out of him and* *enter no more into him! And the spirit cried out, throwing him into convulsions, and came out of him. And he was like one dead, so that many said, He is dead. But Jesus took him by the hand and lifted him up, and he arose. And He entering into a house,* **His disciples asked Him privately, Why could we not cast him out?** *And He said to them,* **THIS KIND can come out by nothing except by PRAYER AND FASTING.** (Mark 9:24-29 MKJV) The Strategy is the same for both because they are the same spirits - pride and unbelief.

Fasting is a strategy in the Spirit - it brings cause and effect into our physical realm. Fasting cleanses our vessels (bodies) and allows us to forsake the **flesh**. This in turn allows us to hear God's voice very clearly. He gives us **UNDERSTANDING** that we previously didn't have - answers come when we fast and we get strategies in the Spirit for breaking strongholds (it also gets rid of the spirits of Pride and Unbelief). God said, **"Starve it out with prayer and Fasting."** This is also a way to get **free from Addictions**.

This is a very important scripture that the Lord wanted me to put here about fasting... *And when you fast,* **do not be like the hypocrites, of a sad face.** *For they* **disfigure their faces so that they may appear to men to fast** (Do not give place to pride and unbelief, when people disfigure their faces in this way, it is an attempt at self-pity - a fruit of pride and unbelief). *Truly I say to you,* **They have their reward** (their 'only reward' is, they may get sympathy from others for their 'sacrifice', instead of trusting that God will reward them). *But you, when you fast, anoint your head and wash your face,* **so that you do not appear to men to fast, but to your Father in SECRET. And your Father who sees in secret shall reward you openly.** (Matthew 6:16-18 MKJV) Wouldn't we all prefer God's reward over an ounce of man's pity? So, **Do Not Tell** others that you are fasting...

What is it that we are supposed to fast? We should leave it up to the Lord - what He wants us to fast, what He wants the fast to be for and how long (ask Him). I did get a Word from the Lord, and

HE IS DECLARING WAR ON THE SPIRIT OF RELIGION! I sensed that when He gave me that word about fasting, it was because He is going to give us a **STRATEGY** and that it was a **STRATEGIC OFFENSIVE BLOW TO THE SPIRIT OF RELIGION.** In effect this word is the strategy. I believe there is more He wants to give us for personal strategies. If we are FREE from the spirit of Pride and Unbelief, Religion can no longer have its hold on us. Some of us will be fasting and praying for others to be free from this spirit and this will bring **PHYSICAL HEALING IN MANY, MANY PEOPLE,** especially those who have illnesses like those that I mentioned above - having to do with the **HEAD, NECK, SPINE, LUNGS** and **STOMACH.** All Glory to our King Jesus, always and forever, amen.

Scripture References

*And when He had come into His own country, He taught them in their synagogue, so much so that they were astonished and said, From where does this man have this wisdom and these mighty works? Is not this the carpenter's son? Is not his mother called Mary? And his brothers, James and Joses and Simon and Judas, and his sisters, are they not all with us? Then from where does this man have all these things? And they were offended in Him. But Jesus said to them, A prophet is not without honor, except in his own country and in his own house. **And He did not do many mighty works there because of their unbelief.** (Matthew 13:54-58 MKJV)*

And He went out from there and came into His native-place. And His disciples followed Him. And when the sabbath day had come, He began to teach in the synagogue. And many hearing Him, were astonished, saying, Where does this one get these things? And what wisdom is this which is given to him, that even such mighty works are done by his hands? Is not this the carpenter, the son of Mary, the brother of James and Joses and Judas and Simon? And are not his sisters here with us? And they were offended at Him. But Jesus said to them, A prophet is not without honor, except in his native-place, and among his own kin, and in his own house. And He could do no work of power there, except *that He laid His hands on a few sick ones, He healed them. **And He marveled because of their unbelief.*** (Mark 6:1-6 MKJV)

The following scripture tells us that if we are giving place to pride when we fast, it is of no cause - it would be better to give to the poor if we cannot humble ourselves during a fast...

*You wonder why the LORD **pays no attention when you go without eating** and **ACT humble.** But on those same days that you give up eating, **you think only of yourselves and abuse your workers.** You even get angry and ready to fight. **No wonder God won't listen to your prayers!** Do you think the LORD wants you to give up eating and to act as humble as a bent-over bush? Or to dress in sackcloth and sit in ashes?* (Many would do these 'religious' things when they fast - if it is done out of 'tradition' or pride, it is pointless.) *Is this really what he wants on a day of worship? I'll tell you what it really means to worship the LORD. Remove the chains of prisoners who are chained unjustly. Free those who are abused! Share your food with everyone who is hungry; share your home with the poor and homeless. Give clothes to those in need; **don't turn away your relatives.** Then your light will shine like the dawning sun, and you will quickly be healed. Your honesty will protect you as you advance, and the glory of the LORD will defend you from behind. When you beg the LORD for help, he will answer, "Here I am!" Don't mistreat others or falsely accuse them or say something cruel. Give your food to the hungry and care for the homeless. Then your light will shine in the dark; your darkest hour will be like the noonday sun. The LORD will always guide you and provide good things to eat when you are in the desert. He will make you healthy. You will be like a garden that has plenty of water or like a stream that never runs dry.* (Isaiah 58:3-11 CEV)

So, the point to the above scripture is that if we are not Mature enough to fast in Secret with a good, even grateful, attitude as Jesus describes above, then we shouldn't fast at all and we should worship Him by doing the things listed in the above scripture...

THE GREAT AWAKENING HAS COME, THE VEIL OF RELIGION IS BEING LIFTED, "I AM WILL CLEAN YOUR HANDS AND RENEW YOUR MIND, REJOICE FOR YOUR REDEMPTION DRAWS NIGH" SALVATION IS HERE & NOW, WE ARE FREE

1/27/2011

The **Truth** is the **Great Equalizer**. The Truth is Bringing the Valleys up higher and the Mountains down lower. It is to one person - their best friend, to another - their worst enemy. But truly, the Truth is always our true friend. Many have been in captivity, in a self-imposed prison, that is the LIE. One thing the Truth will always do is Set Us Free. This is what God desires for ALL of mankind - Freedom! He sent **TRUTH** to the Earth to **FREE us from ALL things,** things that keep us bound, including ourselves. **Freedom is here - we need only to BELIEVE.** Father, I ask that You would give anyone who reads this Word, a desire to know and Understand the Truth, so they may **ALL Finally BE FREE to Free others** who are in need of Your Love through the Truth, in Jesus Name, amen.

And the Lord said, **"A Call for FREEDOM has Come and it is Yours - Yours without shame, without guilt, without fear, without condemnation. You will know you are on the right path, when you see the legalistic spirit of Religion, Jezebel and Poverty, rise up against you. Stand up, Oh Children of Zion and take your places Of Authority and In History. The field is ripe for the Harvest of souls and the Battle Field is set and marked for this battle - this battle that is already WON by My Spirit. You simply Believe and you shall receive - Receive Freedom! Now is the time, Now is the place, for what I have already done for you - through Christ. GIVE it Away to others across the Globe. Take no mind for where your provision comes from, for it comes from ME. I will supply your needs and I will supply your vision as you take the steps of Faith in obedience to My Spirit. Seek Me first, Give and Love, and all that I have promised is yours. Simply obey what I have said** and you shall SEE My Salvation, for a shift in Consciousness based on the TRUTH of My Word is upon you. The veil of religion is being taken away from the eyes of your hearts, HERE AND NOW you ARE FREE to Live, you are FREE to Love, you are FREE to Give, says the Lord of Hosts."

*Then since we have such hope, we use great plainness of speech. And we are not like Moses, who put a veil over his face so that the sons of Israel could not steadfastly look to the end of the thing being done away. (But their thoughts were blinded; **for until the present the same veil remains on the reading of the old covenant, not taken away**.) But this **veil has been done away in Christ**. But **until this day, when Moses is read, the veil is on their heart**. But whenever it **turns to the Lord, the veil shall be taken away**. And the Lord is that Spirit; and **where the Spirit of the Lord is, there IS LIBERTY**. But we all, with our face having been unveiled, having beheld the glory of the Lord as in a mirror, are being changed into the same image from glory to glory, even as by the Lord Spirit.* (2 Corinthians 3:12-18 MKJV)

If there is no liberty (and we have put God in a 45 minute box, in a worship service on Sunday morning), it is not the Spirit of the Lord, it is the spirit of religion. This is having a form of godliness but denying the POWER - His Grace. We need to be Spirit led instead of cowering to the fear of man, especially where the presence of the Lord is concerned. *You who are justified by Law are deprived of ALL effect from Christ; you fell from grace.* (Galatians 5:4 MKJV) *But if you are led by the Spirit, you are not under law.* (Galatians 5:18 MKJV)

And the Lord said, **"I AM will Clean your Hands and Renew your Mind. Freedom IS yours by My Spirit, says the Lord of Hosts."**

And judgment is turned away backward (hindered), *and justice standeth afar off: for truth is fallen* (wavered) *in the street* (an area or broad place), *and equity* (uprightness) *cannot enter* (befall). (Isaiah 59:14 KJV) The prophetic love Truth, Judgment and Justice. These are desires that God has put deep in the spirits of those who are His. This spirit of Religion, Jezebel and Poverty hates the TRUTH and seeks to kill the prophetic voice. Read about Jezebel in the Bible, 1st & 2nd Kings. The scripture above is telling us that when **Truth** wavers (goes back and forth between possibilities), then **Justice** and **Judgment** stand far away from the situation and righteousness cannot enter. This is how the spirit of religion works. It tries to plant a seed of doubt. If this thought or seed is not taken captive unto the obedience of Christ, it can grow into a spirit of Unbelief. Unbelief is rooted in Pride and God resists the proud. *He gives His Grace and Power to the Humble* (1 Peter 5:5 paraphrased).

The spirit of Religion, Jezebel and Poverty (which is rooted in pride - pride and fear is the door by which all other spirits enter) has kept mankind bound since the Garden of Eden. It caused Cain to be in 'competition' with Able. It keeps people bound to the law and Justifying themselves, through their own efforts and works, instead of being **Justified By Faith in Christ, through the GRACE of God.** This has caused people to go after idols and develop a 'survivalist mentality' and a basic distrust for God and others. *For I am not ashamed of the Gospel of Christ, for it is the power of God unto salvation to everyone who believes, to the Jew first and also to the Greek. For in it the righteousness of God is revealed from faith to faith, as it is written, "The JUST* (or Justified) *shall live by faith."* (Romans 1:16-17 MKJV) We are Justified only by faith IN CHRIST and we LIVE by it.

I know it jumps around a little bit, but try to follow the scripture below…

*This means that **everyone who has faith will share in the blessings** that were given to Abraham because of his Faith. **Anyone*** *who tries to please God by obeying the Law is under a curse. The Scriptures say, "Everyone who doesn't obey everything in the Law is under a curse."* (This means that if you try to obey any part of the law, then you are under a curse and you are responsible for ALL of the law. This is an impossible task because it is only by His Grace that we can do anything - even breathe. *If we are trying to obey the law then we have fallen from grace* (Galatians 5:4 paraphrased). This is not what God wants for His people. It is too much of a burden. He wants us to take Him on, His burden is light.) **No one can please God by obeying the Law.** *The Scriptures also say, "The people **God accepts because of their faith will live." The Law isn't based on faith.** It promises life only to people who obey its commands. But **Christ rescued us from the Law's curse,** when he became a curse **in our place.** This is because the Scriptures say that anyone who is nailed to a tree is under a curse. **And because of what Jesus Christ has done, the blessing that was promised to Abraham was taken to the Gentiles.*** (Abraham, by Faith in God, reached beyond the Cross and took a hold of the Promise that hadn't happened yet (in our time line), because he believed God. And also, all who are not of Jewish decent are now Grafted into the Body (of Christ) through FAITH IN CHRIST.) *This happened so that by faith we would be given **the promised Holy Spirit*** (So we can be led by the Spirit just as Abraham was, by faith). *My friends, I will use an everyday example to explain what I mean. Once someone agrees to something, no one else can change or cancel the agreement. That is how it is with the promises **God made to Abraham and his descendant.** The promises were not made to many descendants, but only to one, and **that one is Christ.** What I am saying is that **the Law cannot change or cancel God's promise** that was made 430 years before the Law was given. If we have to obey the Law in order to receive God's blessings, those blessings don't really come to us because of God's promise* (this is saying that if we did something to obtain the promise then it isn't God's promise - His promise was only ratified through the **work of the Cross and only by faith (BELIEF) IN Christ**, not by our works). *But God was kind to Abraham and made him a promise. What is the use of the Law? It was given later to show that we sin. **But it was only supposed to last until the coming of that descendant who was given the promise*** (only meant to be until Jesus came and

174

paid the price to fulfill it). *In fact, **angels gave the Law to Moses, and he gave it to the people** (there was a mediator between God and man). **There is only one God, and the Law did not come directly from him.** (For if the inheritance is of Law, it is no more of promise; but God gave it to Abraham by way of promise. Why then the Law? It was added because of transgressions, until the Seed should come to those to whom it had been promised, **being ordained through angels in the Mediator's hand.** (Galatians 3:18-19 MKJV)) Does the Law disagree with God's promises? No, it doesn't! **If any law could give life to us, we could become acceptable to God by obeying that law. But** the Scriptures say that sin controls everyone, so that **God's promises will be for anyone who has Faith in Jesus Christ.** The Law controlled us and kept us under its power **until the time came when we would have faith.** In fact, **the Law WAS our teacher.** It was supposed to **teach us Until We Had Faith** and were acceptable to God. **But once a person has learned to have faith, there is NO MORE NEED to have the Law as a teacher.*** (Galatians 3:9-25 CEV) So, FAITH IN CHRIST FULFILLS THE LAW...

The Gospel of the Grace of God is the POWER unto Salvation, TRUE SALVATION. He did not do away with the law but He FULFILLED it through our Faith IN HIM. So, if we are not under the law, but under Grace (being Spirit led), then the burden of the law no longer exists and we **ARE FREE IN CHRIST!** What then, is required of us? **We Believe by Faith in Christ Jesus.**

This is how we receive...

*But we are bound to give thanks always to God for you, brothers beloved of the Lord, because God has from the beginning chosen you to **Salvation through Sanctification of the Spirit*** (this is Gods part and it's already DONE, Salvation is for here, not someday, but NOW) *and* (this is our part) ***Belief Of The Truth,** to which He called you by our gospel, to the **Obtaining Of The Glory** of our Lord Jesus Christ.* (2 Thessalonians 2:13-14 MKJV)

Then what about this scripture???

*Do not think that I have come to destroy the Law or the Prophets. I have not come to destroy but to **fulfill*** (satisfy). *For truly I say to you, Till the heaven and the earth pass away, not one jot or one tittle shall in any way pass from the Law until all is fulfilled. Therefore whoever shall relax one of these commandments, the least, and shall teach men so, he shall be called the least in the kingdom of Heaven. But whoever shall do and teach them, the same shall be called great in the kingdom of Heaven. For I say to you that **unless your righteousness shall exceed that of the scribes and Pharisees, you shall in no case enter into the kingdom of Heaven.*** (Matthew 5:17-20 MKJV) We Are Only Righteous **Through Faith IN CHRIST.** The Pharisees had no faith, they only had the law. **The law is for the 'lawless', those who have not understood how to have faith yet. Religion is a 'lawless' spirit.**

So, why the law?

*But the **end of the commandment is love out of a pure heart, and a good conscience, and faith unfeigned,** from which some, having swerved, have turned aside to foolish talking, **desiring to be teachers of the law, neither understanding what they say nor that which they affirm.*** (Where there is a religious spirit there is also NO UNDERSTANDING.) *But we know that the law is good if a man uses it lawfully, knowing this, that the **law is NOT made for a righteous one*** (remember, we are ONLY Righteous through Faith IN Christ), ***but for the LAWLESS** and disobedient, for the ungodly and for sinners, for unholy and profane, for murderers of fathers and murderers of mothers, for manslayers, for fornicators, for homosexuals, for slave-traders, for liars, for perjurers, and anything else that is contrary to sound doctrine, according to the glorious gospel of the blessed God, which was committed to my trust.* (1 Timothy 1:5-11 MKJV)

What is our Part?

*We know that everyone who has been **Born of God does not continue to sin**, but the one born of God guards himself, and **the evil one does not touch him**.* (1 John 5:18 MKJV) *Master, which is the great commandment in the Law? Jesus said to him, You shall **love the Lord your God with all your heart, and with all your soul, and with all your mind**. This is the first and great commandment.* (This is to keep our FOCUS on God and not on other things or people. What we Focus on is what we are Worshiping, what we Worship is what we love, and where our Treasure is there will our heart also be - He wants our hearts in their entirety.) *And the second is like it, You shall **love your neighbor as yourself**. **On these two commandments hang all the Law and the Prophets**.* (Matthew 22:36-40 MKJV) In the New testament, when we read scriptures saying, "Obey My Commands," these are the 'Commands' He is talking about. And this also... *But **if you are led by the Spirit, you are not under law**.* (Galatians 5:18 MKJV) If we have Faith IN Christ, we will grow in these three areas. If we truly live and walk IN these three areas, we will not sin or break any of the 'Ten Commandment Laws'.

The Trinity of Trust in God is Loving God, Loving others and being Spirit led. As we mature in these three areas, sin will not be a thought to us and the enemy cannot touch us because we are not leaving doors open for him. It is not out of our 'performance' but out of our **LOVE** and **RESPECT** for God and others that we do not sin. *For sin shall not have dominion over you, for you are not under Law, but under Grace.* (Romans 6:14 MKJV) The enemy is already defeated. It is only when we Focus on him that he has any power. Remember, what we Focus on becomes our 'God' or 'god'.

Maturity In Christ

GRACE seeks out and fills in the gaps between our limited understanding and the ALL knowing of God. Also, **Pain is the Process of Grace and Power in our lives.** This is when God starts the process of molding us into **'Sons of God'.** When you see the phrase **'Make You Perfect',** in the Bible, He is talking about **MATURITY.** Growing up and becoming Sons of God requires maturity. Part of the process of being mature in Christ, is being able to humble ourselves before God. There are two reasons that this is imperative. The first is because **Humility is the Secret Place, our Place of Protection and Provision.** The second reason is this... When we share the Word of God while pride is still present in our lives, it becomes twisted **by pride,** and pride is what religion and legalism are made up of. It is error and it causes us to be false prophets. It also causes us to judge others with 'wrong judgment', and then manipulate them into salvation by using Fear. We are to give love to them, the Love of Christ - into Faith IN Christ. How can anyone have faith or believe in Christ if all they see from 'God's people' is wrong judgment? Wrong judgment is a fruit of pride and hatred, and hatred is actually murder. *Do not marvel, my brothers, if the world hates you.* **We know that we have passed from death (the law) to life (grace), because we Love the brothers.** *He who does not love his brother* **abides in death.** *Everyone* **hating his brother is a murderer.** *And you know that no murderer has everlasting life abiding in him. By this we have known the love of God, because He laid down His life for us.* **And we ought to lay down our lives for the brothers.** *But whoever has this world's goods and sees his brother having need, and shuts up his bowels from him, how does the love of God dwell in him? My children, let us not love in word or in tongue,* **but in deed and in truth.** (1 John 3:13-18 MKJV) Our **actions speak the truth** about us louder than our words...

To BE the First, we must first, BE the Last...

*He said to Him, Which? Jesus said, You shall not murder, you shall not commit adultery, you shall not steal, you shall not bear false witness, honor your father and mother, and, you shall love your neighbor as yourself. The young man said to Him, I have kept all these things from my youth up; what do I lack yet? Jesus said to him, If you want to be **perfect*** (mature in Christ), *go, sell what you have and give to the poor, and you shall have treasure in Heaven.* **(What are we willing to GIVE UP at the heart level, for the call that Christ has placed on our lives?)** *And come, follow Me* **(Be Spirit led).** *But when the young man heard that saying, he went away sorrowful; for he had great possessions* **(when things 'have' us, it is difficult to enter the Kingdom - He wants us to have the things, not them have us).** *Then Jesus said to His disciples, Truly I say to you that a rich man will with great difficulty enter into the kingdom of Heaven. And again I say to you, It is easier for a camel to go through the eye of a needle than for a rich man to enter into the kingdom of God. When His disciples heard, they were exceedingly amazed, saying,* **Who then can be saved?** *But Jesus looked on them and said to them,* **With men (by our works and 'performing' the Law)** *this is impossible, but with* **God (through Grace - faith in Christ)** *all things are possible. Then answering Peter said to Him, Behold, we have forsaken all and have followed You. Therefore what shall we have? And Jesus said to them, Truly I say to you that you who have followed Me, in the regeneration, when the Son of Man shall sit in the throne of His glory, you also shall sit on twelve thrones, judging the twelve tribes of Israel. And everyone who left houses, or brothers, or sisters, or father, or mother, or wife, or children, or lands, for My name's sake, shall receive a hundredfold, and shall inherit everlasting life.* **But many who are first shall be last; and the last shall be first.** (Matthew 19:18-30 MKJV)

GRACE works Humility in us, so the Gospel Can be effective in our lives...

And the Lord said, **"By My GRACE I will Align ALL things."** He is about to slap the **'Law of GRACE'** on us and we will **ALL** come into **Unity**, not because we will all agree on Doctrine or Denomination, but because He is going to **Perfect** or **Mature** us. We will be 'Growing Up' IN HIM. *But the God of all **grace**, He calling us to His eternal glory by Christ Jesus, **after you have suffered a little**, He will perfect* (mature), *confirm, strengthen, and establish you.* (1 Peter 5:10 MKJV) It takes GRACE to be able to 'grow up'. *When I was an infant, I spoke as an infant, I thought as an infant, I reasoned as an infant. But when I became a man, I did away with the things of an infant.* (1 Corinthians 13:11 MKJV)

As the veil of Religion, Jezebel and Poverty is lifted from the eyes of our hearts, we will see that the HARVEST, the BLESSING and the KINGDOM are already here. This is a change in our Perspective and Perception to the Understanding that we **ARE Already FREE.** It was our blinded Perspective and Perception that caused us to be bound - the veil of Religion, Jezebel and Poverty. Christ **Brought and Bought freedom** for us from sin and death, most of us just have not come to the full understanding of it yet.

The **Spirit of Truth** will sweep the land and **we will see the manifestation of the Sons of God.** *For as many as are **led by the Spirit** of God, they are the **Sons of God.** For you have not received the spirit of bondage again to fear, but you have received the Spirit of adoption by which we cry, Abba, Father! The Spirit Himself bears witness with our spirit that we are the **children of God.** And if we are children, then we are heirs; heirs of God and joint-heirs with Christ; **so that if we suffer with Him, we may also be glorified together** (it is our destiny to 'suffer' with Him, so we can become Sons, so that His Glory may be shown IN and Through us in the Earth). *For I reckon that the sufferings of this present time are not worthy to be compared with the coming glory to be revealed in us. **For the earnest expectation of the creation waits for the manifestation of the Sons of God.*** (Romans 8:14-19 MKJV)

Scripture References

Please read these scriptures - there is more revelation in them...

But none of these things move me, neither do I count my life dear to myself, so that I might finish my course with joy, and the ministry which I received from the Lord Jesus Christ, to testify fully the **gospel of the grace of God.** (Acts 20:24 MKJV)

So, my brothers, you also have become **dead to the law by the body of Christ** *so that you should be married to Another, even to Him raised from the dead, that we should bring forth fruit to God. For when we were in the flesh, the passions of sin worked in our members through the law to bring forth fruit to death. But now we* **having been set free from the Law,** *having died to that in which we were held, so that we serve in* **newness of spirit and not in oldness of the letter.** (Romans 7:4-6 MKJV)

For the promise that he should be the heir of the world was **not to Abraham or to his seed through the Law, but through the righteousness of faith.** *For if they of the Law are heirs,* **faith is made void and the promise is made of no effect;** *because the Law works out wrath, for* **where no law is, there is no transgression.** *Therefore* **it is of faith so that it might be according to grace;** *for the promise to be made* **sure** *to all the seed, not only to that which is of the Law* (the Jews), *but to that also which is of the faith of Abraham, who is the father of us all* (Romans 4:13-16 MKJV)

For where your treasure is, there will your heart be also. (Matthew 6:21 MKJV)

Come to Me all you who labor and are heavy laden, and I will give you rest (heavy burdened from trying to perform the law perfectly), *Take My yoke on you and learn of Me, for I am meek and lowly in heart, and you shall find rest to your souls. For My yoke is easy, and My burden is light.* (Matthew 11:28-30 MKJV)

For the weapons of our warfare are not fleshly, but mighty through God to the pulling down of strongholds, pulling down imaginations and every high thing that exalts itself against the knowledge of God, and bringing into captivity every thought into the obedience of Christ; (2 Corinthians 10:4-5 MKJV)

And Jesus said to him, Foxes have holes, and birds of the air have nests, but the Son of Man has nowhere to lay His head. And He said to another, Follow Me! But he said, Lord, first allow me to go and bury my father. Jesus said to him, Let the dead bury their dead, but you go and proclaim the kingdom of God. And another also said, Lord, I will follow You, but first allow me to take leave of those in my house. And Jesus said to him, No one, having put his hand to the plow and looking back, is fit for the kingdom of God. (Luke 9:58-62 MKJV)

Your boasting (pride) *is not good. Do you not know that a little leaven leavens the whole lump?* (If even part of something is a lie it is ALL a lie.) *Therefore **purge out the old leaven so that you may be a new lump, as you are unleavened*** (by Faith In Christ). *For also Christ our Passover is sacrificed for us.* (1 Corinthians 5:6-7 MKJV)

*Now may the God of peace (who brought again our Lord Jesus from the dead, that great Shepherd of the sheep, through the blood of the everlasting covenant) **make you perfect** (mature) in every good work to do His will, working in you that which is well pleasing in His sight through Jesus Christ, to whom be glory forever and ever. Amen. And I beseech you, brothers, allow the word of exhortation. For I have written a letter to you in few words. Know that our brother Timothy has been set at liberty, with whom, if he comes shortly, I will see you. Greet all those leading you, and all the saints. Those from Italy greet you. **Grace** be with you all. Amen.* (Hebrews 13:20-25 MKJV)

*In that He says, **A new covenant, He has made the first one old.
Now that which decays and becomes old is ready to vanish
away.*** (Hebrews 8:13 MKJV)

*And out of His fullness we all have received, and **grace for grace.** For
the Law came through Moses, but **Grace and Truth came through
Jesus Christ.*** (John 1:16-17 MKJV)

*Then Jesus said to the Jews who believed on Him, If you continue in
My Word, you are My disciples indeed. And you shall **know the
truth, and the truth shall make you free.** They answered Him, We
are Abraham's seed and were never in bondage to anyone. How do you
say, You will be made free? Jesus answered them, Truly, truly, I say to
you, Whoever practices sin is the slave of sin. And the slave **does not
abide in the house forever, but the Son abides forever.** Therefore if
the Son shall make you free, you shall be free indeed.* (John 8:31-36
MKJV) Freedom IS Freedom…

*Owe no man any thing, but to love one another: **for he that loveth
another hath fulfilled the law.*** (Romans 13:8 KJV)

*But whom He predestinated, these He also called; and whom He called,
those He also justified. And whom He justified, these He also glorified.
What then shall we say to these things? **If God is for us, who can be
against us?** Truly He who did not spare His own Son, but delivered
Him up for us all, how shall He not with Him also freely give us all
things? Who shall lay anything to the charge of God's elect? It is God
who justifies.* (Romans 8:30-33 MKJV)

FLOOD WATERS & RAIN SIGNIFY THE FLOOD & RAIN OF BLESSING COMING TO THE MID-WEST, "AMERICA, I WILL RESTORE YOU TO PURITY WITH MY 'NEW FIRE', I WILL HEAL THE WATERS & RESTORE FERTILITY, YOU ARE THE 'NEW WINESKINS'"

6/17/2008, Revised 2/20/2011

The Lord gave me a vision of great floods and heavy rains, winds and tornadoes that would be coming to the Mid-west, in the United States of America. Especially, down the mid-section of the Country and around the Rivers that flow South. I first received this Word in June of 2008 and the Lord told me to release it now.

And the Lord said, **"This is the 'certain destruction' that I have told you would be coming to the United States** (In the 'Provoking Seed' Word). **Things will get worse before they get better. These Floods, Rains, Winds and Tornadoes that you will experience, will be a parallel to the Rain and Flood of Blessing that I am about to release to the United States. It will begin in the 'Heart Land', for True Repentance will always begin with the Heart. Revival will spread across this Great Nation and you will once again be Great in My Eyes. I have seen the rhythm of your deepest hearts intent America. Under the muck, under the sludge and the distractions of this life, your heart has been to honor the One True God Jehovah. I will turn the hearts of you the people of this Great Nation, for when I turn your hearts, they will be turned towards Me and you will know the Truth and the Truth will set you Free. Those who have had their Trust in something besides Me alone, will 'clamor' to find those who I already call Sons** (The Sons of God, are those who have been broken before the Lord and have learned to put ALL of their Hope and ALL of their Trust In God alone). **These are My True Sheep, those who Hear My Voice and obey it. They are the Salt and the Light that has preserved the Earth, those in whom I am well pleased. They are those whom I have already raised up into the True**

Apostolic Anointing and all will know who they are. I need them to be seen and recognized - not for the pride of man, no, but for My purposes in the Earth. They will be set as Pillars, so all can see and find them for they carry the anointing and the Key that will set the captives FREE for My Namesake and for My glory, says the Lord of Hosts."

And the Lord said, **"Many quote the scripture that says - *'He sends rain on the just and on the unjust'*** (Matthew 5:45 paraphrased). **They believe this only to mean something negative, but truly, I say unto you, that the Rain, Floods, Winds and Tornadoes that you will see, is a sign of My Rain and Flood of blessing that is to come, not only in the natural but in the supernatural realm as well."

The overabundance of chaotic weather patterns that we will be seeing, not only throughout the midsection of the United States, but around the globe, has already begun and is a prophetic sign in the earth that God is about to **'rain down'** His Blessing and Power in the earth realm. The blessing that comes is directly proportionate to the amount of chaotic weather that will be seen. The blessing was not dependent on chaotic weather, but the Lord is blessing us in spite of it.

And the Lord said, **"For I will shift and move things on your behalf. I will bring My beauty out in you to be seen by all, even in the midst of chaos and calamity, and multitudes will repent and be set Free. Unusual miracles will begin to take place, especially in the financial arena. Do NOT LIMIT ME on how, when and through whom, I can bless you. If you do, you will be left out. Be Open and be Expecting. Just as an expectant mother, about to give birth, for a season of tremendous blessing is in your midst, so Reach for it and Take it, says the Lord of Hosts."**

Then the Lord spoke just one word to me, **"Water."** I looked up some of the meanings of the word water and one of the main things that water does is, it **brings and sustains life** to the living and it also **Cleanses or Purifies things.** Once, when I was seeking the Lord about the spirit of rebellion, He gave me the revelation of how **obeying** God causes us to **live or have life** and **disobeying** God brings **death.** So, **rebellion is death.** The Lord is saying that especially in this season, He is purging the land from the spirit of Rebellion and Death (this also has a lot to do with the spirit of religion - they are all intertwined with each other).

God is ushering in the spirit of **Water and Life** - the Zoe life and **Grace of God.** Many women will be raised up in this anointing (this does not mean that men will not be a part of it, it just means that we will see more women than ever before being raised up in this time and they will hold high places of authority in the Spirit realm). There will no longer be restrictions placed on women in ministry and they will have the respect that God deems them to have. This is not for their Glory, but for the Glory of God.

Now I would like to mention more about Water... There is **water** and **salt** in our tears. We will **Groan** unto the Lord, with tears (I believe this is also an aspect of the Jeremiah Prophetic Anointing). And the Lord said, **"For I will cause you to Groan unto Me from your spirit man. Only I will be able to understand this groaning, and through you, I will be birthing this 'new life' and 'new fire' into the Earth - especially in the United States, and directly into its Heart-Land."**

The Lord gave my husband and me, a vision of a Principality that is in New Orleans and it flourishes up and down the shores of the Mississippi River. Not only there, but also up and down the shores of all the rivers that flow South. It is positioned there strategically by the enemy, near the **water and life** and it is trying to 'restrict' or 'squeeze' the life out of this Nation. This principality is Python (picture the snake - it has a head, neck, spine, lungs and stomach). This spirit affects the 'head'. Take for instance, the head of a household - it affects men and their ability to understand how to take the head of their household in the proper way with **love** and **understanding.** It also affects a man's ability to understand what it is to be a good leader and what it is to be a man - especially in today's society where many women are in competition with them. It makes man feel insignificant and useless. Also, in the natural it is responsible for ailments that affect the head, neck, spine, lungs and stomach. This includes things like mental illness, depression, Alzheimer's, autism, paraplegics, lung diseases and breathing problems, stomach and intestinal issues, dumbness, deafness, speech problems, cancers of any of these areas and much more. God is dealing with this principality and bringing deliverance to those who have been affected by it.

In the midst of this devastation, the Lord is bringing change and purifying this **'water front'** land. He is giving it a **'face lift'** and healing the land, and in turn, bringing a Revival of **Physical Healing** and **Creative Miracles.** There is a connection between the spirit of Unbelief, Python, and a lack of healing and miracles being made manifest. Unbelief tries to root itself in people's hearts because it knows that **Belief is the Basis of Faith.** In this scripture Jesus shows that our faith is what makes us whole. *And he said unto her, Daughter, be of good comfort: **thy faith hath made thee whole**; go in peace.* (Luke 8:48 KJV)

Faith is an **'action'** word. If we believe at a heart level, to the point where we will **ACT ON** what we Believe, it will become **Faith in Motion.** This is **NOW Faith** and it is **A Substance, NOW!** God revealed to me that the **strategy to be free from the spirit of Unbelief is to Fast and Pray.** (Scriptures to back this up are in the Word called, **"GOD IS DEALING A STRATEGIC OFFENSIVE BLOW TO THE SPIRIT OF RELIGION, "STARVE IT OUT WITH PRAYER AND FASTING"** Matthew 17:13-21, Mark 9:24-29, Matthew 6:16-18 and Matthew 13:54–58).

The Lord reminded me of the scriptures in the Bible that refer to water, to the ground and the womb being barren (2 Kings 2:19 and Proverbs 30:16). And the Lord said, **"For I will bring**

Healing Waters and I will Heal the Waters of this Great Nation. Not only will you see less pollution, you will see an increase of Renewable Energy Sources, new sources, simply because you never knew how to apply them in this way before. Look for three to come on the scene. This will make you a wealthy Nation once again. This will also translate into the human and natural realm and women who had once been barren will now see a surge in fertility rates, especially in the Mid-West and in other parts of the Country near the Water Sources, especially where there are flowing rivers."

This was a specific Word for the United States, but the Lord told me that this is not just happening in the United States, but also around the World where we are seeing these same types of weather patterns - like heavy rains, flooding, tornadoes, earthquakes etc. And the Lord said, **"For My Alignment has come, not only to the Planet Earth, but to your Souls, and Physical Bodies as well."** You see, it is like someone going to a chiropractor to get an adjustment - it seems to feel good at first, but then the true adjustment will come in the following days as your body gets used to the 'New' positioning. And the Lord said, **"For I AM has set this time and this place APART, for you are NOW in a New Position, you are NOW in a New Place of Authority and a New Place of Influence, For YOU ARE THE NEW WINE SKIN."**

The New Wine can Not go into the Old wineskins. God is broadening our thinking because where He wants to take us is a Greater place than any generation before this time. It is a **New Time** and a **New Day** and a **New Beginning.** The old moves of God are not where He wants our minds to be. He said, **"For behold, I do a New thing. No more of this 'fighting your own battles.' Stand in Faith and Belief and SEE the Salvation of your Lord. For I AM will show up BIG on your behalf. If you could 'save yourself' by your works, or even be Justified to the 'naysayers' by trying to stand up for yourself, then, I would not get ALL the Glory. Run into Me, says God, and See Me** move mountains on your behalf. Those who come against My elect will have 'Daddy' to deal with."

For many years, I struggled with religious spirits and bondage. I am actually very grateful now, for the presence of those things in my life. Although, I wasn't too grateful at the time, they taught me, along my path, and helped me to learn how to Trust in the Lord. You see, we can use that which opposes us to help us 'step up' to each new level of Understanding In Him. I believe the **TRUTH will set the Body of Christ FREE! This 'Truth' is the Understanding of His GRACE.** I know it has set me FREE! I am not boasting, but rather testifying to the Freedom that the Lord can bring if we **Dare to Believe** in something other than the 'dogma' that most of us were taught in organized religion. He said, **"I long to set you Free, NOT by your works, but by My Grace alone."**

And the Lord said, **"Although you may be 'going through' right now, do not worry and do not fear, for it is My Hand that is stretching you. I have to stretch you - so You will think of yourselves as a New Wineskin. This stretching has to happen before you can actually be one. What is it that makes you a 'NEW WINESKIN' you ask? It is simply, the Revelation and the Belief of the Truth of the New Covenant. You ARE in fact, 'The NEW' and I am about to pour My 'New Wine' and My 'New Fire' into YOU - My New Wineskins. The more you are stretched the more of My Presence, Light, Heat and Anointing you will be able to hold. I Am is about to Honor you and set you on High. I will Open Door after Door after Door of My Favor and you who have been praying for years for your Family's Salvation, will see them come into the Kingdom One by One. I will 'flood' you in My Presence. There is coming a Great Revolution, a Revolution of LOVE and you will Live and Walk in the Spirit of FREEDOM and that of Truth, says the Lord of Hosts."**

Now back again to the word 'water'... It also means to **dampen.** I looked up the word dampen and the synonyms are the words **reduce** and **diminish.** The Lord is taking the 'Us' out of our hearts. He is reducing or diminishing our 'man's system' (way of doing and thinking), Not only at the head level, but also at the heart level. At the same time, He will rid us of the idols that we have made for ourselves in this Country (USA). He always reduces us when He is about to make Himself **'Big'** in our lives, or when He is about to fill us with more of Him. If we are to be 'full of Him' we cannot be 'full of ourselves'. *When we are weak, He is strong.* (2 Corinthians 13:9 paraphrased)

There are other meanings of the word **water** that the Lord had me look up, and this is what He said, **"I will cause you to soak in, be saturated, be drenched, be inundated, and overwhelmed by My Water and Life anointing. Get ready for Fire and Power. Soak it up, Soak it up, Soak it up! For it will give you strength for the days to come. Receive My Strength, Receive My Flood and I will disparage** (laugh at, mock, belittle, ridicule, pour scorn on) **your enemy. He thought he could take you down, but No! I will crush his head and prosper you America, for I know who you are in your future state, in your repented state and I choose to see you there NOW! I will Honor you, I will lift you up, I will bring your enemies to their knees and they will know who your God is - the One True God Jehovah. This Mid-West Region is about to Explode with My Power. This 'New Fire'** (new meaning innovative or fresh) **that I will send will be Greater than anything you have seen in the Earth before this time. It will spread across this entire Nation and it will not lessen by any means. This will be the 'Spark' that Ignites the Entire Globe on Fire for ME and it will continue on, and Become the End Time Harvest of Souls. You need simply to Obey and Live, Obey and Live, Obey and Live. For America, you are a Great Nation and I will make you a Great and Pure Nation once again, for My Namesake and My Glory, says the Lord of Hosts."**

And then the Lord said, **"Show The Homosexual Community MY True Nature With Unconditional Love. WRONG JUDGMENT IS TRULY HATE AND IT MEANS THAT YOUR FOCUS IS OFF. I will cause the hearts of the gay community to turn and cause them to be tender towards their maker at a later time, in My time. Your responsibility is simply to love them and to not condemn. What makes you think you can be a respecter of persons** (playing favorites) **when I AM is not. You simply show My true nature with unconditional love, to those who you may have rejected in the past. There has been too much of this 'rejecting' going on. My people have thought that they were doing Me a favor, but they were blinded to Truth and not walking in love. Turn away from rejection of any kind coming from your own heart and love ALL people - ALL of them. This is how you can overcome being rejected yourself. Simply accept everyone and do not judge, but Love. Remember, just because someone is 'not saved' in your eyes, does not mean that they will not be My people in the future. YOUR GOD IS NOT LIMITED TO YOUR TIMETABLES. These are My people, for I own it ALL, and loving them is how you will win them for My Kingdom. They are so desperate for love because they have been so rejected. For this reason, they turn to others who have been rejected. They are finding comfort, not from the True Comforter, but they end up finding comfort in the wrong places because no one has shown them My True Unconditional Love yet. I meet everyone right where they are at and love them right where they are at - and into where they will be. I long for My people to do the same, and this is how you will show My glory in the earth. Love for all, at all times, unconditionally, for My Glory and My Namesake, says the Lord of Hosts."**

It is a **Strategy.** Perfect, or Perfected, Love casts out ALL Fear. All sin or unclean spirits, originate from fear and pride (but Love breaks the back of pride). God is love. When we Give Love Or Give God there is deliverance for others, and even ourselves, in it. *There is no fear in love, but perfect love casts out fear, because fear has torment. He who fears has not been perfected in love. We love Him because He first loved us. If anyone says, I love God, and hates his* *brother, he is a liar. For if he does not love his brother whom he has seen, how can he love God whom he has not seen? And we have this commandment from Him, that he who loves God should love his brother also.* (1 John 4:18-21 MKJV)

There is a 'line being drawn in the sand' in the 'church', and a sharp distinction will be made between those who are the Lord's True Sheep and those who are not. His True Sheep will be easily identifiable because of the Love they Give. The religious, judgmental spirit will be seen instantly and it will cause people to be literally sick to their stomach, when it is around them. The hateful, self-focused words will be like someone scratching a chalk board. This spirit will not get its way anymore and it will not be able to deceive those who walk in Truth. ANYTHING, (even if it seems like it is a good thing) that takes our Focus off of God, Christ, or the Cross, is sent as a distraction and is of the Anti-Christ spirit. Do not give it a foothold. We are going to be able to identify these things very quickly, starting in this season. The King of Glory is about to show His Glory in the earth in massive proportions very soon.

The Lord revealed something very important to me. If anyone does not LOVE the TRUTH, they will be deceived by God Himself (God will send them strong delusion and they will be deceived - see the scripture below). If this is the case and God is allowing it, we have to Trust Him In it, not only with our own condition, but also with others conditions as well. We all believe, understand and love different degrees of the Truth, God already knows this. He is faithful and just to finish the good work He has started in us and in others. The Key is for us to be mindful of Ourselves and Our Relationship with God. We should ask the Lord, "How much truth do I love?" He will reveal it to us, and we can work with Him on our own Love of the Truth. The more love for Truth we HAVE, the more our Light will shine in the darkness and light the path for others to see their way to Truth. Our responsibility was never to go and 'save' the world or to Focus on the 'evil' or the 'devil'. It was Jesus' responsibility to save the world and 'It' is Finished! Our part is to Give Love, no matter what someone believes or what their spiritual condition may be. It is not our part to judge others. When they see the light that is in us, and because we loved them and didn't judge them, they will want what we have and follow in the same direction. Eventually, they will Walk in Light and Truth as well. *And then the lawless one will be revealed, whom the Lord shall consume with the breath of His mouth and shall destroy with the brightness of His coming, whose coming is according to the working of Satan with all power and signs and lying wonders, and with all deceit of unrighteousness in those who perish, because they did not receive the love of the truth, so that they might be saved. And for this cause **God shall send them strong delusion, that they should believe a lie, so that all those who do not believe the truth, but delight in unrighteousness, might be condemned.*** (2 Thessalonians 2:8-12 MKJV)

This is a quote from the Word called, **"THE LAST SHALL BE FIRST & THE FIRST SHALL BE LAST, I AM RESHAPING YOUR PAST & CHANGING YOUR TESTIMONY, WITH PHYSICAL HEAT, I WILL ERADICATE POVERTY"** The Lord told me to add it to this Word. And the Lord said, **"Unusual Miracles and Manifestations will begin to take place. Just because you haven't seen it done this way or that way before does not mean that it is not God. Do not judge ANY move of My Spirit, or you will be left out of it. Let Me out of the box and I will show you great and mighty things that you know not of. I will, through the revelation of Total Trust in ME, Renovate, Repair, Restore, Mend, Fix Up, and Refurbish you, for this 'NOW FAITH' season is upon you. For NOW FAITH is 'Substant', NOW! It is NOW FAITH! Get a hold of the fact that it is NOW. Stop believing for somewhere down the road when the river rises and the cattle come home! Your Miracle IS NOW and already exists on the inside of you. It is what My Kingdom is made up of and it wants to be let out! Believe it and you shall see it. Says the Lord of Hosts."**

This is the time when the Lord is pressing us so we can see what is in our hearts, besides Him. The question will be asked... When we are Pressed, what is it that comes out? Love or Pride? Fear or Faith? Are there idols there? When we feel the heat, and we see any fruit of pride, this is a good time to evaluate if there are any idols. For most it is mammon. Look at this scripture, He will not allow us to be tempted beyond our ability to withstand it - this is a good time to look inside our hearts for idols... *So let him who thinks he stands take heed lest he fall. No temptation has taken you but what is common to man; but God is faithful, who will not allow you to be tempted above what you are able, but with the temptation also will make a way to escape, so that you may be able to bear it. Therefore, my dearly beloved, flee from idolatry.* (1 Corinthians 10:12-14 MKJV)

I have seen those whose total belongings and earthly possessions were destroyed by disasters and all that came out of them was gratefulness, it is a beautiful sight to see. You see, **gratefulness is the release that God needs from us to release blessing into our realm.** We need to ask Him to **Create in us a Grateful Heart.** Perhaps if we can work with Him to cultivate this kind of heart in ourselves, we can avoid or avert some of these disasters that are coming...

According to their deeds, accordingly he will repay, fury to his adversaries, recompense to his enemies; to the islands he will repay recompense. So shall they fear the name of the LORD from the west, and his glory from the rising of the sun. **When the enemy shall come in like a Flood, the Spirit of the LORD shall lift up a Standard against him.** *And the Redeemer shall come to Zion, and unto them that turn from transgression in Jacob, saith the LORD. As for me, this is my covenant with them, saith the LORD; My spirit that is upon thee, and my words which I have put in thy mouth, shall not depart out of thy mouth, nor out of the mouth of thy seed, nor out of the mouth of thy seed's seed, saith the LORD, from henceforth and for ever.* (Isaiah 59:18-21 KJV)

UNFORGIVENESS - THE POISON THAT ONLY KILLS THE ONE WHO PROTECTS IT & ONLY BURNS THE ONE WHO HOLDS ON TO IT

4/10/2011

Many of us are walking around with unforgiveness in our hearts. We display it proudly like some kind of badge - we even think we have the 'right' to have and to hold this badge. This is usually because someone perpetrated something against us and, in many cases, it is because of a misunderstanding based on our own wrong judgment of a situation or a person. **Then, we wonder why we are sick or have other things going wrong in our lives.**

Unforgiveness in our own heart does not doom the perpetrator to the pits of hell - it doesn't even necessarily cause them to feel guilty. Unforgiveness in our own hearts only puts us in a self-imposed prison of hate and fear. **It is a poison that only condemns those who hold on to it and protect it with their very lives, literally.** Those who hold onto unforgiveness are playing with fire. I once heard someone say that unforgiveness is like taking poison and expecting the other person to die.

Unforgiveness is **born out of pride** because we are 'telling' the God of the universe who deserves to be forgiven and for what. When we are in pride in any form, we open the door for the enemy to get a foothold into our lives. You see, he knows that if he can get us to TAKE offense, then he can cause us to hold unforgiveness. Holding unforgiveness then traps us in a stagnate and powerless state of fear where we become paranoid about who will offend us next. It causes a basic distrust of all people and this causes disunity. Then, we begin to weigh and measure people based on our own tragic past. The Truth is, if we truly Trusted God, we would know that we do not have to trust other people to Do or Be any certain way. **This type of trust and hope belongs to God alone.** When we finally put out hope and trust in Christ, we are then FREE to truly Love others, no matter what shape they are in and no matter what they have or haven't done. **We are Free to Give, Live, Love and Forgive!**

When we hold unforgiveness we end up just 'surviving' and we are not truly living or being present. Being present in the moment, and not living in the past or the future but being in the now, is where Love, Faith, Peace and God's Presence all reside. In the state of fear that comes from unforgiveness, we will not be effective for anything, let alone the Kingdom of God. **Humility In Christ, is the only safe place there is.** We can get to a place of Maturity and Humility In Christ, where we can Reside and Decide ahead of time, to Not take offense to anything - yes, Anything. **Where there is offense, pride is also present.** Ouch, I know, but this is true. Unforgiveness can also be a form of fear based control - it is actually a manifestation of witchcraft - yes, Witchcraft. If we are in fear in ANY way, then we are not perfected in love. Read 1 John 4:17-21.

We **ALL need to FORGIVE** what we know of, that needs to be forgiven, and ask God if there is anything else that we do not remember. We can ask Him to bring those things back to our remembrance. Many times it will be like living the circumstance all over again - not fun, but in some cases, necessary. Going through this process can also feel very real and painful, but when we finally forgive, it is Us who is FREED FROM THE PRISON OF TORMENT and not the 'other person' (they have to make things right with God themselves because whether we know it or not, if they have sinned and did not repent, they have their own prison that they have made for themselves and they will reap what they have sown). **When we Trust God with Justice and Judgment and pray for our enemies, we will see our lives begin to turn around and we will finally BE FREE In Christ. This is when His Glory will shine in the Earth for all to see. Remember, we could be holding a grudge against God or even ourselves, this needs to be dealt with, in our hearts, as well.**

Scripture References

But to whom you forgive anything, I also forgive. For if I forgave anything, for your sakes I forgave it to him in the person of Christ; so that we should not be overreached by Satan, for we are not ignorant of his devices. (2 Corinthians 2:10-11 MKJV)

And He said to them, When you pray, say: Our Father, who is in Heaven, hallowed be Your name. Your kingdom come, Your will be done, as in Heaven, so also on the earth. Give us day by day our daily bread, and forgive us our sins, for we ourselves also forgive everyone who is indebted to us. And lead us not into temptation, but deliver us from evil. (Luke 11:2-4 MKJV)

Therefore be merciful, even as your Father is merciful. Judge not, and you shall not be judged. Condemn not, and you shall not be condemned. Forgive, and you shall be forgiven. Give, and it shall be given to you, good measure pressed down and shaken together and running over, they shall give into your bosom. For with the same measure that you measure, it shall be measured to you again. (Luke 6:36-38 MKJV)

Therefore I say to you, All things, whatever you ask, praying, believe that you shall receive them, and it will be to you. And when you stand praying, if you have anything against anyone, forgive it so that also your Father in Heaven may forgive you your trespasses. But if you do not forgive, neither will your Father in Heaven forgive your trespasses. (Mark 11:24-26 MKJV)

Peter came up to the Lord and asked, "How many times should I forgive someone who does something wrong to me? Is seven times enough?" Jesus answered: Not just seven times, but seventy-seven times! This story will show you what the kingdom of heaven is like: One day a king decided to call in his officials and ask them to give an account of what they owed him. As he was doing this, one official was brought in who owed him fifty million silver coins. But he didn't have any money to pay what he owed. The king ordered him to be sold, along with his wife and children and all he owned, in order to pay the debt. The official got down on his knees and began begging, "Have pity on me, and I will pay you every cent I owe!" The king felt sorry for him and let him go free. He even told the official that he did not have to pay back the money. As the official was leaving, he happened to meet another official, who owed him a hundred silver coins. So he grabbed the man by the throat. He started choking him and said, "Pay me what you owe!" The man got down on his knees and began begging, "Have pity on me, and I will pay you back." But the first official refused to have pity. Instead, he went and had the other official put in jail until he could pay what he owed. When some other officials found out what had happened, they felt sorry for the man who had been put in jail. Then they told the king what had happened. The king called the first official back in and said, "You're an evil man! When you begged for mercy, I said you did not have to pay back a cent. Don't you think you should show pity to someone else, as I did to you?" The king was so angry that he ordered the official to be tortured until he could pay back everything he owed. That is how my Father in heaven will treat you, if you don't forgive each of my followers with all your heart. (Matthew 18:21-35 CEV)

He IS, that He IS and if we Just BE, we will SEE His Glory! Just Being Present is where His Presence IS - this is also the place where we find Hope, Faith, Peace, Love and Destiny...

Dare to Hope

Dare to Dream

Dare to Believe

Dare to go on Your Own

Journey In
The Prophetic...

A Journey In The Prophetic

Prophetic Words from the Throne of Grace

Visit (or write) me at:

WendyChristie.com (find all the main relevant links here)

Facebook - Wendy Christie, Wendy Christie II

FB Group - A Journey in the Prophetic - Wendy M Christie

FB Fan Page - Wendy M Christie - A Journey in the Prophetic

My Blog - Wendy-Christie.blogspot.com

A Journey In The Prophetic, P.O. Box 8913, Rockford, IL 61126

Try a popular search engine online and search for 'Wendy Christie Journey', without quotes, and you should see several links to choose from on the first page, including Facebook Notes, Wall, and Links, plus Book Order Links and more...

A *Journey* in the Prophetic - *Wendy* M *Christie* | Facebook

Wendy M *Christie* - A *Journey* in the Prophetic | Facebook

————⊂∙⊃————

To order more copies of this book contact your local book store, go online to most major book sites or visit us at WendyChristie.com to get a signed copy (while available). Digital versions are also available.

More books to come!

Visit WendyChristie.com for more details.